THE KITCHEN

FRENCH COOKING

THE KITCHEN LIBRARY
FRENCH COOKING

Caroline Ellwood

OCTOPUS BOOKS

CONTENTS

This edition published 1988 by
Octopus Books Limited
59 Grosvenor Street, London W1

© Cathay Books 1981
ISBN 0 7064 3248 7

Printed in Hong Kong

NOTES
Standard spoon measurements
are used in all recipes
1 tablespoon = one 15 ml spoon
1 teaspoon = one 5ml spoon
All spoon measures are level.

Fresh herbs are used unless otherwise
stated. If unobtainable substitute a
bouquet garni of the equivalent dried
herbs, or use dried herbs instead but
halve the quantities stated.

Use freshly ground black pepper where
pepper is specified.

Ovens should be preheated to the specified
temperature.

For all recipes, quantities are given in both
metric and imperial measures. Follow either set
but not a mixture of both, because they are not
interchangeable.

Ingredients and cooking terms marked with
an asterisk are explained on pages 10-11.

INTRODUCTION

Good food and France are considered to be synonymous. French cuisine is renowned for its excellence and throughout the country, food is treated with the utmost respect. The French house-wife will take as much care in choosing potatoes and onions, as in selecting strawberries and cherries, demanding the freshest produce at all times.

There are two different styles of French cooking: haute cuisine and regional cooking. Haute cuisine is the elaborate, rather expensive style, originally developed by the great French chefs. For economic reasons, it is becoming rare, but is still practised in top restaurants and hotels in Europe and America.

Regional cooking describes the more familiar dishes prepared everyday in family homes, cafés and bistros throughout France. This style of cooking is relatively inexpensive for it employs simple ingre-dients and cooking methods. The recipes in this book reflect this popular type of cooking.

Cooking varies considerably between the regions, the nature of regional dishes being determined mainly by the ingredients available locally. However, quality ingredients, together with subtle flavourings of herbs and seasonings, form the basis of all regional dishes.

Regional Cooking

Normandy has a reputation for good food. Lush cattle pastures and apple orchards provide the region with its specialities: cider, Calvados – an apple-flavoured liqueur, thick cream, butter and a variety of cheeses. Normandy is the home of Camembert, Port Salut and Neufchâtel.

Brittany produces a good crop of early fruit and vegetables, especially mild-flavoured French onions, artichokes and strawberries. Onion sellers, carrying strings of onions on bicycles, are a familiar sight in the region. Fish are caught along Britanny's coastline, especially shellfish: lobsters, crabs and mussels. Crêpes, too, are popular.

In Paris and Ile de France, the Charcuterie windows bulge with delicious terrines, galantines, and duck pâtés. Here too, you can find cooked tripe, crabs, langoustines, scallops, skate, mackerel, shrimps and mussels, and the fine Breton artichokes, leeks and cauliflowers. Dairy produce is brought in from the surrounding regions, notably Brie, from the area south of Orly. Pâtisseries offer a sumptuous selection of French bread, pastries and gâteaux.

Further east, on the German border lie Alsace and Lorraine. These regions share a similar cuisine, which has a germanic flavour: sauerkraut, cheesecakes and Riesling wine are common fare. Charcuteries are packed with homemade sausages, smoked pork and terrines of duck and tongue. Quiche Lorraine must be the most famous dish of the region: crisp light pastry, encasing eggs, cream and filling ingredients – normally cheese, onions and bacon.

Further south lies Burgundy, thought by some to be the gastronomic heart of France and renowned for its wines, especially Chablis, Beaune, Mâcon and Beaujolais. The area prides a wealth of foods, particularly chickens, beef, a variety of game and freshwater fish, snails, mushrooms and edible fungi.

Nearby Lyonnaise has a good reputation for food. The locally grown onions are used for traditional dishes, such as *Pommes Lyonnaise* and *Soupe a l'Oignon*. The adjacent province, Savoie, borders on Switzerland and is ostensibly influenced by its neighbouring cuisine. Here excellent smoked and salted sausages can be bought, as well as the locally made cheeses – Beaufort, Tomme and Emmenthal.

Traversing to the west coast, one reaches the Dordogne and the land of *fois gras*. Geese are fattened for this delicately flavoured liver, and goose fat is used for frying. Périgord is the home of the highly prized truffle. From December through to January trained dogs and pigs search for truffles in the woods. In the Gironde estuary where the

Dordogne enters the sea, sturgeons are caught to provide the finest caviar in the world. To the south lie the vineyards of Bordeaux; these yield quality wines, such as Medoc, Graves and Sauternes.

In the south-west corner of France lie the provinces of Bearnaise and Basque. An abundance of sweet peppers, Bayonne hams, home-made *saucisses* and maize are a reminder of the proximity of Spain. Sardines, squid, prawns and other shellfish are caught along the coastline.

Languedoc, the large southern province, shares the Mediterranean seaboard with Provence, and a similar cuisine. However, the region retains an identity of its own, evident in such culinary delights as *cassoulet* and Roquefort cheese – produced from sheep's milk.

Provence, with its Italian influence, is a profusion of fresh fruits, vegetables, olives, garlic and herbs. From the olive groves comes the olive oil, which characterises Provençal cooking. Fish soups and stews are prepared all along the coastline, from a seemingly endless variety of species displayed in the markets.

Important Ingredients in French Cooking

The following list explains those ingredients which are considered most important in French cuisine.

Cheese *(Fromage)*: Parmesan, Gruyère and Roquefort are the most frequently used cheeses in French cooking. For a cheeseboard, there is a wide selection of French cheeses obtainable in this country, including various types of Brie, Camembert, Neufchâtel, Boursin, Tome-au-Raisin and Bleu–de–Bresse.

Garlic *(Ail):* This is an essential flavouring in many soups, sauces, casseroles, roasts and salads, particularly those of Provence. The strength of the garlic flavour depends upon how it is used. A cut garlic clove rubbed around a salad bowl will impart a mild flavour whereas cooking brings out the flavour strongly.

Herbs *(Herbes)*: Parsley, tarragon, bay and thyme are the most frequently used herbs in French cooking. Chervil and chives are also used in season, especially for soups and salads. Basil, fennel and oregano are Provençal flavourings.

Mushrooms *(Champignons)*: The French use a wide variety of mushrooms including cépes, girolles and boletus. These

Selection of French cheeses illustrated below: Rambol pepper, Crediou with herbs and garlic, Coeurmandie, Crediou with hazelnuts, Saint Julien with walnuts, Neufchâtel, Camembert.

varieties are not generally available fresh in this country but they can be obtained in a dried form.

Mustard *(Moutarde):* A popular condiment in French cooking; the most common type being the tarragon mustard of Dijon. Often herbs and whole mustard grains are added to give a coarse-textured mustard.

Olive Oil *(Huile d'olive):* Nothing really compares with the flavour of good quality olive oil. The most delicious olive oil is the rich green variety obtained from the first olive pressing; it is expensive and therefore usually reserved for salad dressings. Ordinary olive oil is suitable for most cooking purposes. For deep-frying corn oil is better.

Shallot *(Echalotes):* These are extensively used in French cooking. If shallots are unobtainable button onions can be used instead, or the white part of spring onions.

Vinegar *(Vinaigre):* Red or white wine vinegars are used for all cooking purposes; malt vinegar is not found in French cooking. Homemade vinegars are often flavoured with herbs, especially tarragon, or garlic.

Wine *(Vin):* Cooking in wine enhances the flavour of food. Normally only one or two glasses of reasonably good wine are required. The wine is almost always reduced, either by long slow cooking, or by rapid boiling.

Glossary of Cooking Terms

Aioli: A mayonnaise from Provence: crushed garlic cloves, blended with egg yolks and olive oil. Served with cold fish, meat or vegetables.

Bain–Marie: A water bath, used for gentle cooking. The dish in which the food is to be cooked is placed in a roasting tin, containing water. This is kept at simmering point or just below. Used for pâtés and egg custards.

Baste: To spoon hot fat or liquid over food as it roasts, to keep it moist and succulent.

Beurre Manié: Equal parts of butter and flour, kneaded together to form a paste and used to thicken soups, sauces and casseroles. The casserole must be below boiling point when the beurre manié is added, a little at a time, beating thoroughly after each addition until incorporated. The casserole is then brought to the boil to thicken.

Blanch: To plunge food into boiling water for a short time, normally up to 2 minutes. Used to facilitate peeling, e.g. green peppers, tomatoes.

'Blind', To bake: To cook a pastry case without its filling. The case is lined with greaseproof paper and dried beans to prevent the base rising.

Bouquet Garni: A small bunch of mixed herbs, tied together with thread. It is used to flavour dishes during cooking and extracted afterwards. A bouquet garni normally consists of a bay leaf, 2 or 3 parsley sprigs and a thyme sprig.

Clarify: To remove impurities. To clarify butter: melt, allow to settle, then strain through muslin. Stock for a consommé or aspic jelly, may be clarified by the addition of egg whites and egg shells. The liquid is whisked while coming to the boil, then strained through muslin.

Croûtes: Pieces of bread toasted or fried. Used as a base or garnish for savoury dishes. The bread may be cut into various shapes, e.g. hearts, rounds or triangles.

Croûtons: Tiny cubes of fried or toasted bread, used as a garnish for soups.

Deglazé: To detach sediment in a roasting dish in which meat has been cooked, so it can be used to enhance the flavour of sauces or gravy. A little stock or wine is added to the pan, while scraping to incorporate the sediment.

Fines Herbes: A mixture of herbs: parsley, chervil, chives and tarragon.

Infuse: To extract flavour by immersing flavouring ingredients in a liquid. Herbs and vegetables are steeped in warm stock or milk to flavour soups and sauces.

Marinate: To soak meat, fish, fruit or vegetables in a liquor for at least a few hours to impart flavour and tenderise. The liquor, or marinade, is usually wine, a mixture of oil and vinegar, or a liqueur.

Poach: To cook food in liquid just below boiling point.

Praline: Caramelized sugar with almonds. Often crushed into a powder and used in soufflés, creams and ices.

Reduce: To reduce the volume of a liquid by boiling, uncovered. Used to thicken sauces, stocks or syrups and concentrate flavour.

Roux: Equal quantities of butter and flour cooked together and used as the basis for most white and brown sauces.

Sauté: To toss food in a little butter or oil over low heat until the fat is absorbed, or over high heat until the food is browned.

Vanilla sugar: Vanilla flavoured sugar, made by putting a broken vanilla pod into a jar of sugar. The jar should be sealed for the sugar to absorb the vanilla flavour.

Preparing aioli

STOCKS & SAUCES

Fonds Blanc de Veau
White Veal Stock

Use for soups, white sauces, light sautéed dishes, stews, etc.

*1 kg (2 lb) stewing
veal
1-1.5 kg (2-3 lb)
veal bones, in
small pieces
(optional)
2 large onions,
quartered
1 large carrot
2 celery sticks
1 large bouquet
garni*
1 bay leaf
8 peppercorns
2 cloves
½ head of garlic
cloves, unpeeled
2.25 litres (4 pints)
water
salt*

Place the veal and bones, if using, in a large saucepan, cover with cold water and bring to the boil. Drain and rinse out the pan. Return the veal and bones to the pan, add the remaining ingredients, with salt to taste, and bring to the boil. Skim the surface, cover and simmer for 3 to 4 hours, skimming occasionally.

Cool slightly, then strain. Taste, and if a more concentrated flavour is required, boil until the stock is slightly reduced. Cool quickly, then skim any fat from the surface.

Store, covered, in the refrigerator for up to 3 days, or in the freezer for up to 3 months. Use as required.
Makes about 1.75 litres (3½ pints)

Fonds Brun
Brown Stock

Use for making brown soups and sauces; beef, lamb and game stews.

1 kg (2 lb) stewing
  veal or beef
1-1.5 kg (2-3 lb)
  beef or veal bones,
  in small pieces
  (optional)
50 g (2 oz) butter
2 large onions,
  chopped
few pieces of onion
  skin
2 carrots
2 celery sticks
1 large bouquet
  garni*
8 peppercorns
½ head of garlic
  cloves, unpeeled
2.25 litres (4 pints)
  water
2 tablespoons tomato
  purée
salt

Put the meat and bones, if using, in a roasting pan and cook in a preheated hot oven, 220°C (425°F), Gas Mark 7, for 30 to 35 minutes, until browned on all sides.

Melt the butter in a pan, add the onions and fry until browned. Add the meat, bones and remaining ingredients, with salt to taste. Bring to the boil and skim the surface. Cover and simmer for 3 to 4 hours, skimming occasionally.

Cool slightly, then strain. Allow to cool, then skim any fat from the surface.

Store in the refrigerator for up to 3 days, or in the freezer for up to 3 months. Use as required.

**Makes about 1.75 litres
  (3½ pints)**

Fumet de Poisson
Fish Stock

Use for fish soups, sauces and poaching fish.

25 g (1 oz) butter
1 large onion,
   chopped
1 kg (2 lb) fish
   trimmings (bones,
   skin, heads, etc.)
1.2 litres (2 pints)
   water
1 bouquet garni*
6 peppercorns
300 ml (½ pint) dry
   white wine
1 bay leaf
salt and pepper

Melt the butter in a pan, add the onion and cook until just beginning to colour. Remove from the heat and add the remaining ingredients, with salt and pepper to taste. Return to the heat and bring to the boil. Simmer, uncovered, for 30 minutes, skimming the surface occasionally; do not boil or the flavour will be spoiled.

Cool slightly, then strain and check the seasoning. Store, covered, in the refrigerator for up to 2 days. Use as required.

Makes about 1.25 litres (2¼ pints)

Sauce Brun
Brown Sauce

6 tablespoons
   clarified butter*
1 large onion,
   chopped
2 carrots, chopped
2 celery sticks,
   chopped
2 rashers bacon,
   derinded and diced
50 g (2 oz) plain
   flour
1-1.2 litres (1¾-2
   pints) Fonds Brun
   (see page 13) or
   beef stock
1 bouquet garni*
2 tablespoons tomato
   purée
salt and pepper

Melt the butter in a pan, add the onion, carrots, celery and bacon and cook for 10 minutes. Add the flour and cook, stirring, until golden.

Remove from the heat and gradually stir in the fonds brun or beef stock. Add the bouquet garni, tomato purée, and salt and pepper to taste. Bring to the boil and simmer for 1½ to 2 hours, until the sauce is thick enough to coat the back of a spoon. Check the seasoning, remove the bouquet garni, and use as required.

Makes about 1.2 litres (2 pints)

Sauce de Tomates

Tomato Sauce

2 tablespoons olive
  oil
1 clove garlic, crushed
1 onion, chopped
2 rashers streaky
  bacon, derinded
  and chopped
750 g (1 ½ lb)
  tomatoes, chopped
salt and pepper
2 teaspoons chopped
  basil

Heat the oil in a pan, add the garlic
and onion and fry for 10 minutes
until soft, but not coloured. Add the
bacon, tomatoes, and salt and pepper
to taste. Cover and cook for 30 to 35
minutes.

Purée in an electric blender, then
strain, or rub through a sieve. Check
the seasoning and add the basil.
Serve as required.
Serves 4 to 6

15

Sauce Béchamel

300 ml (½ pint)
  milk
2 slices onion
1 bay leaf
6 peppercorns
1 small carrot
1 parsley sprig
40 g (1½ oz) butter
40 g (1½ oz) plain
  flour
salt and white pepper

Put the milk in a saucepan and add
the onion, bay leaf, peppercorns,
carrot and parsley. Bring to the boil
and remove from the heat at once.
Cover and leave until cool to allow
the flavours to infuse.

Melt the butter in a pan, stir in the
flour and cook, stirring, for 2 minutes.
Strain the milk and gradually add to
the pan, stirring. Bring to the boil
and cook for 2 minutes. Season to
taste with salt and white pepper.
Makes a generous 300 ml (½ pint)

Sauce Soubise

65 g (2½ oz) butter
750 g (1½ lb)
  onions, sliced
25 g (1 oz) plain
  flour
300 ml (½ pint)
  Fonds Blanc de
  Veau (see page
  12) or milk
150 ml (¼ pint)
  double cream
salt and pepper
pinch of nutmeg

Melt 50 g (2 oz) of the butter in a
pan, add the onions and cook until
soft, but not coloured. Stir in the
flour and cook for 1 minute.

Gradually add the *fonds blanc de
veau* or milk, stirring constantly.
Bring to the boil and cook for 2
minutes. Stir in the cream, and salt
and pepper to taste. Simmer for 1
minute.

Add the nutmeg and remaining
butter and serve immediately.
Makes a generous 300 ml (½ pint)

Sauce Duxelles

125 g (4 oz)
  mushrooms
3 shallots
25 g (1 oz) butter
150 ml (¼ pint) dry
  white wine
450 ml (¾ pint)
  Sauce Brun (see
  page 14)
2 tablespoons tomato
  purée
salt and pepper
3 tablespoons chopped
  mixed herbs

Chop the mushrooms and shallots
finely.

Melt half the butter in a pan, add
the mushrooms and shallots and
cook for 5 minutes. Stir in the wine
and cook until reduced by half. Stir
in the *sauce brun*, tomato purée, and
salt and pepper to taste. Remove
from the heat and stir in the
remaining butter and herbs. Serve
immediately, with roast or grilled
beef or lamb.

Makes about 600 ml (1 pint)

Sauce Mornay

50 g (2 oz) Gruyère
  cheese, grated
25 g (1 oz) Parmesan
  cheese, grated
300 ml (½ pint) hot
  Sauce Béchamel
French mustard

Add the cheeses to the hot *sauce
béchamel* and stir until melted; do not
reheat. Stir in mustard to taste. Serve
immediately.

Makes a generous 300 ml (½ pint)

Sauce Velouté

25 g (1 oz) butter
25 g (1 oz) plain
  flour
450 ml (¾ pint)
  Fonds Blanc de
  Veau (see page 12)
  or chicken stock
salt and pepper

Melt the butter in a pan, stir in the
flour and cook for 1 minute.
Gradually stir in the *fonds blanc de
veau* or chicken stock. Season with
salt and pepper to taste. Bring to the
boil and cook for 2 minutes; the
sauce should not be too thick.

Makes about 450 ml (¾ pint)

SOUPS & STARTERS

Soupe à l'Oignon
Onion Soup

50 g (2 oz) butter
1 kg (2 lb) onions, sliced
1.2 litres (2 pints) Fonds Brun (see page 13) or beef stock
salt and pepper
6 slices French bread, toasted
125 g (4 oz) Gruyère cheese, grated

Melt the butter in a pan, add the onions and fry very gently until golden, stirring occasionally; this may take 30 to 40 minutes. Add the *fonds brun* or beef stock, and salt and pepper to taste. Bring to the boil, cover and cook for 20 minutes.

Sprinkle the toast with the cheese. Place under a preheated grill until golden brown.

Divide the soup between individual bowls and top each with a slice of toast. Serve immediately.

Serves 6

Potage Crème de Cresson
Cream of Watercress Soup

40 g (1½ oz) butter
2 onions, chopped
350 g (12 oz)
    watercress
40 g (1½ oz) plain
    flour
1.2 litres (2 pints)
    Fonds Blanc de
    Veau (see page
    12) or chicken
    stock
salt and pepper
2 egg yolks
150 ml (¼ pint)
    double cream
watercress sprigs to
    garnish

Melt the butter in a pan, add the onions and cook until soft, but not browned. Add the watercress and cook for 5 minutes until softened. Stir in the flour and cook for 2 minutes. Gradually stir in the *fonds blanc de veau* or chicken stock, bring to the boil and cook for 5 minutes. Season to taste with salt and pepper.

Sieve or work in an electric blender until smooth. Return to the pan.

Beat the egg yolks and cream together, then gradually add 300 ml (½ pint) of the hot soup, stirring constantly. Return to the pan and cook for 1 to 2 minutes; do not boil.

Pour into a tureen and garnish with watercress.
Serves 6

Potage Crème au Crabe
Cream of Crab Soup

50 g (2 oz) butter
250 g (8 oz) onions,
  sliced
750 g (1 ½ lb)
  tomatoes, chopped
1 bouquet garni*
150 ml (¼ pint) dry
  white wine
750 ml (1 ¼ pints)
  Fumet de Poisson
  (see page 14)
300 g (10 oz) cooked
  fresh, or canned,
  crabmeat
1 clove garlic, crushed
strip of lemon rind
salt and pepper
150 ml (¼ pint)
  double cream
chopped parsley to
  garnish

Melt the butter in a pan, add the onions and fry for 5 minutes, without browning. Add the tomatoes, bouquet garni, wine, *fumet de poisson*, half the crabmeat, the garlic and lemon rind. Season with salt and pepper to taste. Bring to the boil, cover and simmer for 30 minutes. Remove the bouquet garni and lemon rind.

Sieve or work in an electric blender until smooth. Return to the pan and stir in the remaining crabmeat. Heat gently and stir in the cream.

Serve immediately, garnished with parsley.

Serves 4 to 6

NOTE: Use a bouquet garni of thyme, marjoram, basil and parsley, if possible.

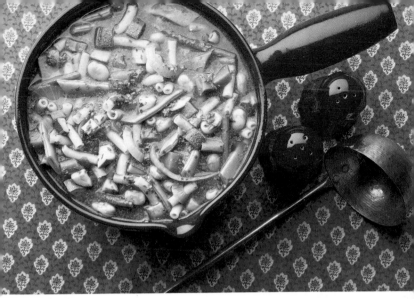

Pistou
Provençal Vegetable Soup

250 g (8 oz)
  courgettes
125 g (4 oz) leeks
500 g (1 lb)
  tomatoes, skinned
175 g (6 oz) carrots
500 g (1 lb) onions
250 g (8 oz) young
  runner beans
250 g (8 oz) French
  beans
250 g (8 oz) shelled
  broad beans
1.2 litres (2 pints)
  Fonds Blanc de
  Veau (see page
  12) or chicken
  stock
salt and pepper
125 g (4 oz)
  short-cut macaroni
PESTO:
4 cloves garlic
12 basil sprigs
4 tablespoons olive oil
TO SERVE:
50 g (2 oz) Parmesan
  cheese, grated

Chop the courgettes, leeks, tomatoes, carrots and onions and place in a large pan, with the remaining vegetables. Add the *fonds blanc de veau* or chicken stock, and season to taste with salt and pepper. Bring to the boil, cover and simmer for 15 minutes. Add the macaroni and cook for 10 to 12 minutes.

Meanwhile, make the pesto. Put the garlic and basil in a mortar and pound to a paste. Add the oil, drop by drop. Remove the soup from the heat and slowly stir in the pesto.

Ladle into a tureen or individual bowls, sprinkle with Parmesan cheese and serve immediately.

Serves 6

NOTE: When fresh basil is unobtainable, omit the pesto and add 2 cloves crushed garlic and 1 tablespoon chopped parsley to the soup, with the stock.

Crème Vichyssoise
Chilled Potato and Leek Soup

50 g (2 oz) butter
6 large leeks,
    chopped
500 g (1 lb)
    potatoes, chopped
900 ml (1½ pints)
    chicken stock
salt and pepper
grated nutmeg
284 ml (10 fl oz)
    single cream
TO GARNISH:
croûtons*
chopped chives

Melt the butter in a pan, add the leeks and cook for about 10 minutes. Add the potatoes, stock, and salt, pepper and nutmeg to taste. Bring to the boil, cover and simmer for 40 to 45 minutes, until the vegetables are tender.

Sieve or work in an electric blender until smooth. Check the seasoning, stir in the cream and chill for 3 to 4 hours.

Serve chilled, garnished with croûtons and chives.
Serves 4 to 6

22

Maquereaux au Vin Blanc
Mackerel in White Wine

300 ml (½ pint) dry
   white wine
150 ml (¼ pint)
   water
1 onion, sliced
1 fennel sprig
strip of lemon rind
6-7 peppercorns
2 bay leaves
salt
2 large mackerel,
   boned
2 teaspoons French
   mustard
2 tablespoons
   chopped parsley
fennel leaves to
   garnish

Put the wine, water, onion, fennel, lemon rind, peppercorns, bay leaves and a pinch of salt in a pan. Bring to the boil and simmer for 10 minutes. Cool, then strain.

Poach the mackerel in this liquid for 10 to 15 minutes. Cool, then strain, reserving half the stock. Arrange the fish on a serving dish.

Mix the reserved stock with the mustard and spoon over the fish. Sprinkle with parsley. Chill before serving, garnished with fennel.
Serves 4

Champignons à la Grecque
Marinated Mushrooms

3 tablespoons olive
   oil
4 shallots, chopped
4 tomatoes, skinned
   and chopped
4 peppercorns,
   crushed
6 coriander seeds
1 bay leaf
1 thyme sprig
salt
500 g (1 lb) button
   mushrooms
4 tablespoons dry
   white wine
2 tablespoons tomato
   purée
chopped parsley to
   garnish

Heat the oil in a pan, add the shallots and fry until soft. Add the tomatoes, peppercorns, coriander seeds, herbs, and salt to taste. Stir in the mushrooms and wine, cover and simmer for 10 minutes.

Transfer the mushrooms to a serving dish. Discard the herbs. Bring the cooking liquor to the boil and boil for 5 minutes until well reduced. Add the tomato purée and spoon over the mushrooms. Sprinkle with parsley and chill before serving.
Serves 4

Crudités

1 head of fennel
juice of ½ lemon
3-4 tomatoes, sliced
¼ cucumber, cut into
    strips
1 celery heart, sliced
½ small cauliflower,
    broken into florets
125 g (4 oz) broad
    beans
2 courgettes, sliced
1 red pepper, cored,
    seeded and sliced
1 green pepper, cored,
    seeded and sliced
AIOLI:
4 cloves garlic
2 egg yolks
300 ml (½ pint)
    olive oil
salt and pepper
1-2 tablespoons wine
    vinegar
TO GARNISH:
chopped parsley
chopped chives

First, make the aioli (garlic
mayonnaise): Crush the garlic in a
mortar to a smooth paste. Add the
egg yolks, one at a time, beating well
with a wire whisk. Add the oil, drop
by drop, whisking constantly until
thickened, then add the remaining oil
in a steady stream, whisking all the
time. Add salt, pepper and vinegar to
taste.
  Cut the fennel into quarters and
toss in the lemon juice. Arrange on a
serving plate with the remaining
vegetables.
  Sprinkle the aioli with the parsley
and chives. Serve with the
vegetables.
Serves 4 to 6
NOTE: Any fresh, crisp vegetables
may be used for this hors d'oeuvre.

Oeufs en Gelée à l'Estragon
Eggs in Tarragon Jelly

4 eggs
1 × 411 g
    (14½ oz) can
    consommé
6 tarragon sprigs
2 slices Parma ham
    or raw smoked
    ham, trimmed and
    halved (optional)
4 tarragon leaves to
    garnish

Boil the eggs for 5 to 6 minutes.
Remove from the pan, cool in cold
water, then shell.
  Put the consommé in a pan with
the tarragon sprigs; heat gently to
simmering point. Remove from the
heat and leave to infuse for 15
minutes, then remove the tarragon.
  If using the ham, wrap a piece
around each egg. Place the eggs in
individual ramekin dishes. Spoon
over the consommé and float a
tarragon leaf on top. Chill until set.
  Serve with Melba toast.
Serves 4

24

Moules Niçoises
Mussels with Herb Butter

*2.75 litres (5 pints)
    fresh mussels*
*2 glasses dry white
    wine*
2 cloves garlic
*6 parsley sprigs,
    chopped*
*6 basil sprigs,
    chopped (optional)*
*50 g (2 oz) butter,
    softened*
*2 tablespoons grated
    Parmesan cheese*
*basil or parsley sprigs
    to garnish*

Put the mussels in a pan, pour over the wine and bring to the boil. Cook until the shells have opened, discarding any that do not open. Strain the liquor through muslin. Crush the garlic in a mortar, add the herbs and pound. Add the butter and cheese; pound to a smooth paste.

Discard the empty half shell from each mussel. Spread the remaining mussel shell with the herb butter and arrange the shells on individual ovenproof dishes. Moisten with a little of the strained liquor.

Brown under a preheated hot grill. Serve at once, garnished with basil or parsley.
Serves 4

Salade Niçoise

½ crisp lettuce
3 eggs, hard-boiled
1 × 397 g (14 oz)
    can artichoke
    hearts
1 × 198 g (7 oz)
    can tuna fish
1 × 49 g (1¾ oz)
    can anchovy fillets
250 g (8 oz)
    tomatoes, skinned
    and quartered
125 g (4 oz) French
    beans, cooked
8-10 black olives,
    stoned
1-2 teaspoons capers
1 tablespoon chopped
    parsley
DRESSING:
2 tablespoons lemon
    juice
4 tablespoons olive oil
1 clove garlic, crushed
pinch of sugar
salt and pepper
scant ½ teaspoon
    French mustard

Line a serving bowl with the lettuce.

Cut the eggs into quarters. Drain the artichoke hearts, tuna and anchovy fillets and arrange in the prepared bowl, together with the remaining salad ingredients.

Put the dressing ingredients in a screw-topped jar and shake well. Pour over the salad, toss well and serve immediately.

Serves 4 to 6

Rillettes de Porc

1 kg (2 lb) belly pork, boned and derinded
salt and pepper
350 g (12 oz) pork fat
2 cloves garlic, crushed
2 teaspoons chopped mixed herbs
2 tablespoons white wine

Rub the meat well with salt and leave to stand for 6 hours.

Cut the meat and fat into small cubes and sprinkle with the garlic, herbs, wine, salt and pepper to taste.

Mix well, then pile into an ovenproof dish. Cover and cook in a preheated cool oven, 140°C (275°F), Gas Mark 1, for 4 hours.

Turn into a sieve over a bowl, to drain off the fat; reserve. Shred the meat and spoon into a serving dish. Pour over enough reserved fat to give a thin layer. Chill until set.

Remove from the refrigerator 1 hour before needed. Serve with French bread.

Serves 8 to 10

Galantine de Porc

2.25 kg (5 lb) hand of pork, bones and rind removed and kept
1 pig's trotter, split
8 shallots
2 cloves garlic
2 tomatoes
3 celery sticks
1 leek, chopped
2 bay leaves
1 bouquet garni*
piece of lemon rind
4 juniper berries, crushed
300 ml (½ pint) dry white wine
salt and pepper
2 egg whites, beaten
2 egg shells
parsley sprigs to garnish

Secure the pork with string and place in a pan with the bones, rind and trotter. Add the remaining ingredients, except the egg whites and shells. Cover with water, bring slowly to the boil, skim, cover and simmer for 2½ hours.

Take out the pork. Simmer for a further 1 hour. Strain the liquid into a bowl and leave until set; skim off the fat. Chop the meat and pack into a terrine. Season liberally with salt and pepper. Chill.

Place the jelly in a pan with the egg whites and shells. Gradually bring to the boil, whisking. Cool for 10 minutes. Strain through muslin to produce a clear stock. Spoon 3 tablespoons over the meat. Pour the remaining stock into a dish and allow to set, then chop.

Turn the galantine onto a serving dish and surround with the jelly.

Garnish with parsley. Serve sliced.

Serves 8

Pâté de Canard
Duck Pâté

*250 g (8 oz) streaky
  bacon rashers*
*250 g (8 oz) belly
  pork, minced*
*1 × 1.75 kg (4 lb)
  duck, boned and
  chopped*
*250 g (8 oz) pork
  fillet, chopped*
*250 g (8 oz) chicken
  livers, chopped*
1 egg, beaten
1 clove garlic, crushed
2 tablespoons brandy
*1 teaspoon dried
  mixed herbs*
pinch of mixed spice
*pinch of ground
  allspice*
*grated rind of 1
  orange*
salt and pepper

Remove the rind from the bacon and arrange in a rectangular ovenproof dish, stretching the rashers to fit if necessary. Mix the remaining ingredients together in a large bowl, adding salt and pepper to taste. Spoon into the dish and spread evenly. Cover with a lid, or buttered greaseproof paper and foil. Place in a *bain-marie** and bake in a preheated moderate oven, 180°C (350°F), Gas Mark 4, for 2 hours.

Put a weight on the top and leave to cool. Chill for 48 hours before serving, sliced, with crusty bread or hot buttered toast.
Serves 8 to 10

Terrine de Campagne
Country Pâté

*500 g (1 lb) streaky
    bacon rashers*
*125 g (4 oz) fresh
    white breadcrumbs*
2 eggs
*150 ml (¼ pint) dry
    red wine*
2 cloves garlic, crushed
*350 g (12 oz) belly
    pork, minced*
*350 g (12 oz) pork
    livers, chopped*
*500 g (1 lb) chicken
    livers, chopped*
*1 teaspoon each
    chopped thyme
    and sage*
*1 tablespoon chopped
    parsley*
grated nutmeg
salt and pepper
parsley sprigs to garnish

Remove the rind from the bacon rashers and use half to line the base and sides of a large terrine or loaf tin, stretching them to fit if necessary. Chop the rest of the bacon and mix with the remaining ingredients, adding nutmeg, salt and pepper to taste.

Turn into the prepared dish, press down firmly and cover with buttered greaseproof paper and foil. Place in a *bain-marie** and bake in a preheated moderate oven, 160°C (325°F), Gas Mark 3, for 2 to 2½ hours.

Place a weight on top of the terrine and leave to cool, then chill. Turn out and garnish with parsley. Serve sliced, with melba toast.
Serves 10 to 12

Soufflé au Fromage
Cheese Soufflé

25 g (1 oz)
  Parmesan cheese,
  grated
25 g (1 oz) Gruyère
  cheese, grated
300 ml (½ pint)
  Sauce Béchamel,
  (see page 16)
4 large eggs,
  separated
pinch of cayenne
  pepper

Grease a 900 ml (1½ pint) soufflé dish. Add the cheeses to the hot *sauce béchamel* and stir over low heat until melted. Remove from the heat, cool slightly, then stir in the egg yolks and cayenne pepper.

Whisk the egg whites until stiff. Carefully fold into the cheese mixture. Spoon into the soufflé dish.

Cook in a preheated moderately hot oven, 200°C (400°F), Gas Mark 6, for 25 minutes until well risen and golden brown. Serve immediately.
Serves 4

Pipérade

1 tablespoon olive oil
1 large onion, sliced
4 green peppers, cored, seeded and sliced
750 g (1 ½ lb) tomatoes, skinned and chopped
1 clove garlic, crushed
salt and pepper
1 tablespoon chopped basil
4 small gammon rashers
4 eggs, beaten

Heat the oil in a frying pan, add the onion and fry until soft. Add the peppers, tomatoes, garlic, and salt and pepper to taste. Cook until the tomatoes are pulpy. Add the basil.

Meanwhile, cook the gammon under a preheated moderate grill until tender, turning once. Place on a warmed serving dish and keep warm.

Add the eggs to the frying pan and stir until just scrambled. Remove from the heat and pile on top of the gammon. Serve immediately.

Serves 4

Gâteau de Crêpes à la Florentine

Cheese, Spinach and Mushroom Crêpe Layer

BATTER:
250 g (8 oz) plain
  flour, sifted
300 ml (½ pint)
  milk
150 ml (¼ pint)
  water
4 eggs
½ teaspoon salt
50 g (2 oz) butter,
  melted
FILLING:
25 g (1 oz) butter
2 shallots, chopped
250 g (8 oz)
  spinach, blanched*
  for 2 minutes and
  drained
salt and pepper
450 ml (¾ pint)
  Sauce Mornay
  (see page 17)
125 g (4 oz) button
  mushrooms
1 clove garlic,
  crushed
113 g (4 oz) cottage
  cheese
1 egg, beaten

To make the batter, put the flour in a bowl and gradually beat in the remaining ingredients. Continue beating until smooth. Cover and chill for 2 hours.

Lightly oil a 16–18 cm (6½–7 inch) frying pan and place over moderate heat. Pour in just enough batter to cover the base of the pan. Cook until the underside is golden, then turn and cook the other side. Repeat with the remaining batter, stacking the cooked crêpes interleaved with greaseproof paper; keep warm.

To make the filling, melt half the butter in a pan, add the shallots and fry until soft. Stir in the spinach, and salt and pepper to taste; cook for 5 minutes. Stir in 3 tablespoons of the sauce.

Melt the remaining butter in a small pan, add the mushrooms and garlic and fry gently until softened. Allow to cool, then stir into the cottage cheese. Add the egg with 3 tablespoons of the sauce; mix well.

Place a crêpe in a greased ovenproof dish and spread with some of the spinach mixture. Top with a crêpe and cover with some of the mushroom mixture. Repeat the layers until all the ingredients are used, finishing with a crêpe.

Spoon over the remaining *sauce mornay*. Cover with foil and bake in a preheated moderate oven, 180°C (350°F), Gas Mark 4, for 25 to 30 minutes, until golden. Cut into wedges and serve immediately.
Serves 4 to 6

Omelette Fines Herbes

6 large eggs, beaten
salt and pepper
2 tablespoons
    chopped mixed
    herbs, (e.g.
    parsley, tarragon,
    chives, chervil)
50 g (2 oz) butter
TO GARNISH:
parsley sprigs
knob of butter

Season the eggs with salt and pepper, add half the herbs and stir well.

Melt the butter in a large omelet pan. When sizzling, stir in the eggs. Lower the heat and tilt the pan, moving the cooked mixture towards the centre with the back of a fork.

When the omelet is set and browned underneath, sprinkle the remaining herbs over the surface, fold in half and slide onto a warmed serving dish.

Garnish with parsley and a knob of butter and serve immediately.
Serves 4

Omelette aux croûtons
Sauté 1 chopped onion and 125 g (4 oz) diced bacon in a little butter. Prepare and cook the omelette as above, omitting the herbs. Top with the bacon and onion mixture and 4 tablespoons croûtons*.

Fold in half and slide onto a warmed serving dish. Garnish with parsley and serve immediately.

35

Boulettes de Semoule
Semolina and Potato Gnocchi

500 g (1 lb)
 potatoes, boiled
 and mashed
salt and pepper
grated nutmeg
450 ml (¾ pint)
 creamy milk
75 g (3 oz) fine
 semolina
2 eggs, beaten
50 g (2 oz)
 Parmesan cheese,
 finely grated
50 g (2 oz) butter,
 melted
75 g (3 oz) Gruyère
 cheese, grated

Season the potatoes liberally with salt, pepper and nutmeg. Mix well and gradually beat in the milk.

Return to the saucepan and heat gently. Stir in the semolina and cook over a low heat, stirring constantly, until the mixture is very stiff and leaves the sides of the pan. Remove from the heat and stir in the eggs and Parmesan cheese. Turn into a greased tin, cover and leave overnight.

Cut the mixture into 2.5 cm (1 inch) squares and, with floured hands, roll into cork shapes. Cook, a few at a time, in boiling salted water for 3 to 4 minutes until they rise to the surface. Remove with a draining spoon and arrange in a greased ovenproof dish. Pour over the butter and sprinkle with the Gruyère cheese.

Bake in a preheated moderate oven, 160°C (325°F), Gas Mark 3, for 15 to 20 minutes. Serve hot.
Serves 4

Tarte à l'Oignon
Onion and Cream Tart

PASTRY:
*125 g (4 oz) plain
   flour
½ teaspoon salt
50 g (2 oz) butter
1 egg, beaten
1-2 teaspoons iced
   water*
FILLING:
*50 g (2 oz) butter
750 g (1½ lb)
   onions, sliced
3 egg yolks
250 ml (8 fl oz)
   double cream
salt and pepper
grated nutmeg*

Sift the flour and salt together into a bowl. Rub in the butter until the mixture resembles fine breadcrumbs. Mix in the egg and sufficient water to make a pliable dough. Wrap in foil and chill for 1 to 2 hours.

Melt the butter in a pan, add the onions and fry gently for about 30 minutes until golden brown. Cool. Beat the egg yolks and cream together, adding salt, pepper and nutmeg to taste. Add the onions and mix well.

Roll out the pastry very thinly and use to line a 20 cm (8 inch) flan tin. Fill with the onion mixture. Bake in a preheated moderately hot oven, 200°C (400°F), Gas Mark 6, for 30 to 40 minutes. Serve hot.
Serves 4 to 6

Quiche au Roquefort

PASTRY:
175 g (6 oz) plain
  flour
½ teaspoon salt
75 g (3 oz) butter
2-4 tablespoons iced
  water
FILLING:
25 g (1 oz) butter
75 g (3 oz)
  Roquefort cheese
50 g (2 oz) ripe
  Camembert
  cheese, crust
  removed
175 g (6 oz) cream
  cheese
3 tablespoons double
  cream
2 eggs, beaten
1 tablespoon chopped
  chives
salt and pepper

Sift the flour and salt into a bowl and
rub in the butter until the mixture
resembles fine breadcrumbs. Mix in
sufficient water to give a soft dough.
Form into a ball; do not knead or
chill. Lightly press into the base and
sides of a 20 cm (8 inch) flan tin.
Prick the base with a fork. Bake
blind* in a preheated moderately hot
oven, 200°C (400°F), Gas Mark 6, for
20 minutes.

Meanwhile make the filling. Beat
the butter until soft, then beat in the
cheeses. Add the cream, eggs, chives,
and salt and pepper to taste. Mix
well and spoon into the prepared
case. Return to the moderately hot
oven and cook for 20 to 25 minutes,
until golden brown and risen. Serve
immediately.
Serves 4 to 6

Gougère

300 ml (½ pint)
  milk
50 g (2 oz) butter
1 teaspoon salt
125 g (4 oz) plain
  flour
4 eggs
125 g (4 oz)
  Gruyère cheese,
  grated
milk to glaze

Place the milk, butter and salt in a
pan. Bring to the boil, remove from
the heat and beat in the flour.

Add the eggs, one at a time,
beating until a shiny smooth paste is
formed. Stir in 75 g (3 oz) of the
cheese.

Using a piping bag fitted with a
2.5 cm (1 inch) plain nozzle, pipe the
mixture onto a greased baking sheet,
to form an 18 cm (7 inch) ring.
Carefully pipe the remaining mixture
on top, making a deep-edged ring.

Sprinkle with the remaining
cheese. Brush with milk and bake in
a preheated moderately hot oven,
190°C (375°F), Gas Mark 5, for 40 to
45 minutes until well risen and
golden. Serve hot or cold.
Serves 6

FISH

Coquilles St. Jacques à la Provençal
Scallops with Garlic and Parsley

75 g (3 oz) butter
3 cloves garlic
12 fresh scallops,
   shelled, or frozen
   scallops, thawed
2 tablespoons
   chopped parsley
salt and pepper

Melt the butter in a pan, add the garlic and fry until browned; discard.

Add the coral and white scallop flesh to the pan and cook for 5 minutes. Sprinkle in the parsley, and salt and pepper to taste. Pile into warmed individual serving dishes and serve immediately.
Serves 4

Truite aux Amandes
Trout with Almonds

4 trout, cleaned, with
  heads and tails
  intact
salt and pepper
75 g (3 oz) butter
50 g (2 oz) flaked
  almonds
juice of 1 lemon
TO GARNISH:
lemon slices
parsley sprigs

Season the fish with salt and pepper. Melt the butter in a frying pan, add the trout and fry for 6 minutes on each side until golden and cooked through. Arrange on a warmed serving dish and keep hot.

Fry the almonds in the butter remaining in the pan until golden. Add the lemon juice and spoon over the fish. Garnish with lemon and parsley and serve immediately.
Serves 4

Moules à la Marinière

50 g (2 oz) butter,
    softened
6 shallots, finely
    chopped
1 bouquet garni*
    (parsley, thyme,
    bay leaf)
450 ml (¾ pint) dry
    white wine
salt and pepper
3.5 litres (6 pints)
    mussels, scrubbed
    clean
25 g (1 oz) plain
    flour
chopped parsley to
    garnish

Melt half the butter in a pan, add the shallots and fry gently until golden. Add the bouquet garni, wine, and salt and pepper to taste.

Bring to the boil, add the mussels, cover and simmer for about 5 minutes until the shells open; discard any that do not. Remove the mussels from the pan with a draining spoon and pile into a warmed serving dish. Keep hot.

Bring the sauce to the boil and boil until reduced by half. Remove the bouquet garni.

Blend the remaining butter with the flour, divide into small pieces and gradually add to the stock, stirring until dissolved. Bring to the boil, stirring, then simmer for 2 minutes. Pour over the mussels and sprinkle with parsley.

Serves 6

Sole Véronique

750 g (1½ lb) sole
    or plaice fillets,
    skinned
2 shallots, chopped
1 sprig parsley
1 bay leaf
150 ml (¼ pint) dry
    white wine
1 tablespoon lemon
    juice
salt and pepper
15 g (½ oz) butter
2 tablespoons plain
    flour
5 tablespoons milk
    (approximately)
1 tablespoon cream
175 g (6 oz) grapes,
    halved, deseeded
    and skinned

Fold the fillets in half and arrange in a buttered ovenproof dish. Sprinkle with the shallots, parsley, bay leaf, wine, lemon juice, and salt and pepper to taste. Add just enough water to cover the fish.

Cook in a preheated moderate oven, (180°C (350°F), Gas Mark 4, for 15 to 20 minutes until tender. Transfer the fillets to a warmed serving dish, using a slotted spoon. Keep warm. Strain the stock.

Melt the butter in a pan, stir in the flour and cook for 1 minute. Gradually stir in the stock and enough milk to make a smooth pouring sauce. Adjust the seasoning and stir in the cream and grapes. Spoon over the fish and serve immediately.

Serves 4

Crevettes au Xérès
Prawns in Sherry

50 g (2 oz) butter
1 clove garlic, crushed
1 small onion, finely
    chopped
salt and pepper
150 ml (¼ pint)
    medium dry sherry
300 ml (½ pint)
    double cream
750 g (1½ lb) cooked
    shelled prawns
TO GARNISH:
chopped parsley
1 cooked unshelled
    prawn (optional)

Melt the butter in a frying pan, add the garlic and onion and fry until softened but not browned. Season with salt and pepper to taste. Pour in the sherry. Bring to the boil and boil until most of the liquid has evaporated. Add the cream and simmer until thickened. Check the seasoning and stir in the prawns.

Pile the mixture into a serving dish, sprinkle with parsley and garnish with a whole prawn if using. Serve immediately.
Serves 6

44

Filets de Poisson Pochés au Vin Blanc

Fish Poached in White Wine

50 g (2 oz) butter
2 tablespoons chopped spring onions
1.25 kg (2½ lb) sole or plaice fillets, skinned
salt and pepper
1 small bunch of parsley
450 ml (¾ pint) dry white wine
2 tablespoons plain flour
125 g (4 oz) cooked shelled prawns
TO GARNISH:
lemon wedges
few cooked unshelled prawns (optional)

Melt half the butter in a pan, add the spring onions and cook for 2 minutes.

Roll up the fish fillets and arrange in an ovenproof dish. Sprinkle with the spring onions, and salt and pepper to taste. Add the parsley and wine. Cover and cook in a preheated moderate oven, 160°C (325°F), Gas Mark 3, for 15 to 20 minutes until tender. Transfer the fish to a warmed serving dish using a slotted spoon and keep warm; reserve the stock.

Combine the remaining butter and flour to make a *beurre manié**. Strain the stock into a pan and bring to the boil. Gradually stir in the *beurre manié* to thicken the sauce. Add the prawns and check the seasoning. Spoon over the fish and garnish with lemon wedges and whole prawns, if using.

Serves 6

La Bouillabaisse
Mediterranean Fish Stew

Use a selection of the following for contrast in textures and flavours: cod or haddock, plaice or sole, red or grey mullet, bream or mackerel, scallops or mussels, crab and prawns.

*1.5 kg (3 lb) assorted
  fish, cleaned*
*2 tablespoons olive
  oil*
*1 large onion,
  chopped*
2 leeks, chopped
*4 cloves garlic,
  crushed*
*500 g (1 lb)
  tomatoes, skinned
  and chopped*
1 bay leaf
1 bouquet garni*
*300 ml (½ pint) dry
  white wine*
few saffron strands
salt and pepper
*1 loaf French bread,
  sliced and toasted*
*chopped parsley to
  garnish*

Remove the heads, bones and skin from the fish; put these in a pan and cover with water. Bring to the boil and simmer for 15 minutes. Strain and reserve the stock. Cut the fish into pieces.

Heat the oil in a large pan, add the onion and leeks and fry until golden. Add the garlic, tomatoes, herbs and wine. Add the fish except the prawns and crab. Pour in the stock, adding water to cover if necessary. Add saffron, salt and pepper to taste. Bring to the boil, cover and simmer for 10 minutes. Add the prawns and crab; cook for 2 minutes.

Arrange the toast in the base of a large tureen or dish, lift the fish from the pan and pile on top. Boil the stock rapidly for 2 minutes, then strain over the fish. Sprinkle liberally with parsley and serve at once.
Serves 6 to 8

Harengs Lyonnaise
Herrings Lyonnaise

50 g (2 oz) butter
2 large onions, sliced
*2 tablespoons plain
  flour*
salt and pepper
4 herrings, cleaned
*2 tablespoons dry
  white wine*
*2 tablespoons
  chopped parsley*

Melt the butter in a pan, add the onions and fry until golden. Drain on kitchen paper.

Season the flour with salt and pepper and use to coat the herrings. Fry in the fat remaining in the pan until well browned. Arrange on a warmed serving dish.

Return the onions to the pan and pour in the wine. Bring to the boil and cook for 2 minutes. Sprinkle in the parsley, then pour over the herrings. Serve immediately.
Serves 4

MEAT

Tournedos Rossini
Fillet Steaks in Madeira Sauce

50 g (2 oz) butter
125 g (4 oz) button
   mushrooms, finely
   chopped
1 × 113 g (4 oz)
   can pâté de foie,
   cut into 2.5 cm
   (1 inch) rounds
4 tablespoons
   Madeira
salt and pepper
1 × 397 g (14 oz)
   can artichoke
   hearts
6 fillet steaks,
   2.5 cm (1 inch)
   thick

Melt half the butter in a pan, add the mushrooms and fry until golden. Transfer to a heatproof dish with the pâté. Spoon over half the Madeira and season with salt and pepper to taste. Place over a pan of hot water to heat through gently. Heat the artichokes in a small pan, then drain.

Season the steaks with salt and pepper to taste. Melt the remaining butter in a pan, add the steaks and cook for 2 to 4 minutes on each side, according to taste.

Arrange the artichoke hearts and steaks on a warmed serving dish. Spoon over the mushrooms, the liquor and remaining Madeira. Place a slice of pâté on each steak and serve immediately, with a selection of vegetables.

Serves 6

Entrecôte à la Moutarde
Steak with Mustard Cream Sauce

750 g-1 kg (1½-
  2 lb) piece sirloin
  steak, 5 cm
  (2 inches) thick
3 tablespoons French
  mustard
salt and pepper
50 g (2 oz) butter
284 ml (10 fl oz)
  double cream
3 tablespoons brandy
watercress sprigs to
  garnish

Spread each side of the steak with
1 tablespoon mustard. Cover and
leave for 1 hour. Season to taste with
salt and pepper.

Melt the butter in a heavy-based
frying pan, add the steak and seal
both sides quickly over high heat.
Lower the heat and cook for 7 to 12
minutes on each side, according to
taste. Transfer to a warmed serving
dish and keep hot.

Add the remaining mustard and
half the cream to the pan, stirring
well to incorporate the meat juices.
Heat gently. Add the remaining
cream and salt and pepper to taste
and bring to just below boiling
point. Add the brandy and stir well.

Cut the steak into serving portions
and pour over the sauce. Garnish
with watercress and serve
immediately, with sauté or chipped
potatoes.
Serves 4 to 6

Steak au Poivre

2 tablespoons green
   peppercorns, or 1
   tablespoon black
   peppercorns
4 rump or fillet
   steaks, each
   weighing about
   150 g (5 oz)
salt
50 g (2 oz) butter
2 tablespoons brandy
150 ml (¼ pint)
   double cream
watercress sprigs to
   garnish

Crush half the peppercorns and rub into the steaks. Season to taste with salt. Melt the butter in a large frying pan, add the steaks and fry quickly on both sides until browned. Cook for 3 to 5 minutes on each side, according to taste. Pour over the brandy, remove from the heat and ignite; when the flames have died down, arrange the steaks on a warmed serving dish.

Add the cream to the pan and cook, without boiling, for 1 minute. Add the remaining peppercorns. Spoon over the steaks, garnish with watercress and serve immediately.

Serves 4

Boeuf à la Bourguignonne

175 g (6 oz) streaky
   bacon, derinded
   and chopped
2 large onions,
   chopped
1.25 kg (2½ lb)
   piece boned and
   rolled topside or
   sirloin of beef
1 bouquet garni*
3 tablespoons olive
   oil
300 ml (½ pint) dry
   red wine
1 tablespoon beef
   dripping or lard
1½ tablespoons plain
   flour
2 cloves garlic,
   crushed
salt and pepper
250 g (8 oz) button
   mushrooms
12 baby onions
1 tablespoon chopped
   parsley to garnish

Put the bacon, chopped onions and beef in a dish. Add the bouquet garni, oil and wine and stir well. Leave to marinate for 4 hours.

Remove the bacon, onions, meat and bouquet garni and drain well. Strain the marinade and set aside.

Melt the dripping or lard in a flameproof casserole. Add the bacon and onion and fry gently for 5 minutes; remove and set aside.

Add the meat to the fat remaining in the casserole and brown well on all sides. Stir in the flour and cook for 1 minute. Stir in the marinade and bring to the boil. Add the bouquet garni, garlic, and salt and pepper to taste. Cover and cook in a preheated moderate oven, 160°C (325°F), Gas Mark 3, for 1½ to 2 hours.

Return the bacon and onion to the casserole, add the mushrooms and whole onions and cook for 1 hour. Remove the bouquet garni.

Serves 6

Pot au Feu

This provides two dishes: a meat course and a soup.
Traditionally the soup is served the following day as a
consommé, garnished with croûtons, or as a thick soup,
with pasta or rice added.

1 kg (2 lb) knuckle
  of veal, cut in half
750 g (1½ lb) leg of
  lamb, cut in half
1 kg (2 lb) leg of
  beef, boned and
  rolled
few meat bones
  (optional)
2 cloves garlic, sliced
3 onions, unpeeled
500 g (1 lb) carrots,
  halved
500 g (1 lb) leeks,
  cut into chunks
4 celery sticks,
  halved
1 small turnip, cut
  into chunks
1 bouquet garni*
2 bay leaves
1 wine glass white
  wine
salt and pepper
TO SERVE:
horseradish sauce
pickled gherkins
olives
capers
mustard

Tie the meat firmly with string to
keep its shape during cooking. Place
in a large saucepan with the bones, if
using. Add the garlic, vegetables,
bouquet garni and bay leaves. Pour
in the wine and sufficient water to
cover. Add salt and pepper to taste.
Bring to the boil, cover and simmer
very gently for 4 hours.

Take out the meat and vegetables
and transfer to a warmed serving
dish. Slice the meat and serve with
the vegetables, horseradish sauce,
pickled gherkins, olives, capers and
mustard.

Leave the soup until cold, then
skim the fat from the surface. To
serve, bring to the boil, strain and
check the seasoning.

Serves 8

Carbonnades à la Flamande
Beef and Onions Braised in Beer

1.5 kg (3 lb) piece
   chuck steak, 1 cm
   (½ inch) thick
salt and pepper
2 tablespoons plain
   flour
2 tablespoons oil
750 g (1½ lb)
   onions, sliced
4 cloves garlic,
   crushed
300 ml (½ pint)
   Fonds Brun (see
   page 13) or beef
   stock
600 ml (1 pint) beer
1 tablespoon brown
   sugar
1 bouquet garni*
2 teaspoons wine
   vinegar
1 tablespoon chopped
   parsley

Cut the steak into 10 × 5 cm
(4 × 2 inch) strips. Season the flour
and use to coat the meat.

Heat the oil in a large pan, add the
meat and fry until lightly browned
on all sides; remove from the pan.

Add the onions to the pan and
cook until golden brown. Return the
meat to the pan and add the garlic,
fonds brun or beef stock, beer, and salt
and pepper to taste. Bring to the
boil, then add the sugar and bouquet
garni.

Transfer to a casserole and cook in
a preheated moderate oven, 160°C
(325°F), Gas Mark 3, for about
2½ hours, until the meat is very
tender. Remove the bouquet garni
and stir in the vinegar.

Transfer to a warmed serving dish
and sprinkle with parsley. Serve with
buttered noodles.
Serves 6 to 8

Cassoulet de Toulouse à la Ménagère

Beans with Pork, Lamb and Sausages

300 g (10 oz) salt
    pork, cut into
    1 cm (½ inch)
    cubes
1 onion
1 bouquet garni*
2 cloves garlic,
    crushed
1 kg (2 lb) haricot
    beans, soaked in
    water overnight
    and drained
salt and pepper
500 g (1 lb)
    Toulouse or other
    pork sausages
1.25 kg (2½ lb)
    piece pork sparerib
    or blade-bone
1.25 kg (2½ lb)
    piece boned
    shoulder of lamb
8 tablespoons fresh
    white breadcrumbs
    (approximately)

Put the salt pork, onion, bouquet garni, garlic and beans in a large saucepan. Add salt and pepper to taste and water to cover. Bring to the boil, cover and simmer for 1¼ hours. Add the sausages and cook for a further 20 minutes.

Meanwhile, roast the pork and lamb in a preheated moderate oven, 160°C (325°F), Gas Mark 3, for about 1½ hours, until tender.

Drain the bean mixture, reserving the liquid; discard the onion and bouquet garni. Put half the beans in a deep ovenproof dish.

Cut the sausages into 2.5 cm (1 inch) lengths, and cut the pork and lamb into serving pieces. Arrange the sausages over the beans and top with the meat. Spoon over 4 to 5 tablespoons of the reserved liquid. Put the remaining beans on top and cover with a 1 cm (½ inch) layer of breadcrumbs. Cook in a preheated cool oven, 140°C (275°F), Gas Mark 1, for 1 hour.

Stir the breadcrumb crust into the beans and meat and add more of the reserved liquid if the cassoulet seems too dry. Sprinkle with the remaining breadcrumbs and return to the oven for 1 hour until the crust is golden. Serve hot.

Serves 10 to 12

Porc Farci aux Pruneaux
Pork Stuffed with Prunes

1.5 kg (3 lb) piece pork fillet salt and pepper 175 g (6 oz) large prunes 25 g (1 oz) seedless raisins ½ teaspoon ground mixed spice 1 tablespoon chopped sage 300 ml (½ pint) dry white wine 2 tablespoons redcurrant jelly 150 ml (¼ pint) double cream parsley sprigs to garnish	Season the pork with salt and pepper and lay flat. Soak the prunes and raisins in boiling water for 30 minutes. Drain well and stone the prunes. Mix the spice and sage with the prunes and raisins. Spread over the meat, leaving a 2.5 cm (1 inch) border. Roll up and secure with string. Place in a roasting pan and pour over half the wine. Cook in a preheated moderately hot oven, 190°C (375°F), Gas Mark 5, for 1½ hours or until tender. Transfer to a warmed serving dish. Add the remaining wine to the roasting pan, place over a low heat and bring to the boil. Simmer for 3 to 4 minutes until reduced to 150 ml (¼ pint). Add the redcurrant jelly and cream, check the seasoning and simmer until thickened. Garnish the meat with parsley. Serve with courgettes and the sauce. **Serves 6**

Côtes de Porc Vallée d'Auge
Grilled Pork Chops with Cider Sauce

4 shallots, chopped 2 tablespoons chopped parsley salt and pepper 4 pork chops 25 g (1 oz) butter, melted 150 ml (¼ pint) dry cider 1 tablespoon Calvados (optional) sage leaves to garnish	Mix the shallots and parsley together, with salt and pepper to taste. Score the chops on both sides and spread with the mixture. Spoon over a little butter. Cook under a preheated medium grill for about 15 minutes on each side until tender. Transfer the chops to a frying pan. Drain off any excess fat from the grill pan and pour the juices over the chops. Add the cider and boil for 2 minutes until the liquor has reduced. Stir in the Calvados, if using. Transfer to a warmed serving dish and garnish with sage. **Serves 4**

Côtelettes en Cuirasses
Lamb Cutlets in Pastry

4 large lamb cutlets
salt and pepper
15 g (½ oz) butter
75 g (3 oz)
   mushrooms, finely
   chopped
125 g (4 oz) chicken
   livers, finely
   chopped
1 clove garlic, crushed
1 tablespoon red
   wine
1 tablespoon chopped
   parsley
¼ teaspoon mixed
   dried herbs
1 × 368 g (13 oz)
   packet frozen puff
   pastry, thawed
1 egg, beaten
TO GARNISH:
sautéed mushrooms
rosemary sprigs

Season the lamb cutlets with salt and pepper. Cook under a preheated grill for 10 to 12 minutes until golden. Drain on kitchen paper; allow to cool.

Melt the butter in a pan, add the mushrooms, livers, garlic, wine, herbs, and salt and pepper to taste. Cook for 10 minutes, then increase the heat until the liquid has evaporated. Cool.

Roll out the pastry and cut into 15 cm (6 inch) squares. Place a little mushroom mixture in the middle of each square, place a cutlet on top and spread with the remaining mixture.

Brush the pastry edges with egg, then wrap around each cutlet. Press the edges together to seal. Place on a baking sheet and brush with egg.

Bake in a preheated hot oven, 220°C (425°F), Gas Mark 7, for 15 to 20 minutes until golden. Serve immediately, garnished with mushrooms and rosemary.
Serves 4

Gigot de Pré-Salé, Farci
Stuffed Shoulder or Leg of Lamb

1.5 kg (3 lb) boned
   shoulder or leg of
   lamb
2 cloves garlic
2-3 large rosemary
   sprigs, broken into
   pieces
2 teaspoons chopped
   sage
8 tablespoons
   chopped parsley
1 tablespoon chopped
   thyme
2 teaspoons chopped
   rosemary
4 shallots, finely
   chopped
1/4 teaspoon ground
   ginger
salt and pepper

Lay the lamb, skin side down, on a
board. Slice 1 garlic clove and crush
the other. Put half the rosemary in a
roasting pan.

Put the crushed garlic, chopped
herbs, shallots, ginger, and salt and
pepper to taste in a bowl and mix
well. Spread over the lamb and roll
up, enclosing the stuffing completely.
Secure with string. Make small
incisions in the surface of the lamb
and insert the garlic slices. Lay the
remaining rosemary on top.

Cook in a preheated moderate
oven, 180°C (350°F), Gas Mark 4, for
1½ hours; the meat should be pink
inside.

Serve with sautéed potatoes,
tossed in parsley.
Serves 6 to 8

Sauté de Veau Marengo
Veal Stew

1 kg (2 lb) stewing
  veal
flour for coating
salt and pepper
2 tablespoons oil
2 onions, chopped
6 tablespoons dry
  white vermouth
300 ml (½ pint) dry
  white wine
500 g (1 lb)
  tomatoes, skinned,
  seeded and chopped
2 tablespoons tomato
  purée
1 teaspoon each
  chopped basil and
  oregano
strip of orange rind
2 cloves garlic, crushed
250 g (8 oz) button
  mushrooms
chopped basil to
  garnish (optional)

Cut the veal into 2.5 cm (1 inch) cubes. Season the flour with salt and pepper and use to coat the veal. Heat the oil in a pan, add the veal and fry until browned on all sides. Transfer to a flameproof casserole. Add the onions to the pan and fry until golden. Add to the casserole, with the remaining ingredients. Bring to the boil, then cook in a preheated moderate oven, 160°C (325°F), Gas Mark 3, for about 2 hours, until tender. Remove the orange rind.

Garnish with basil, if using. Serve with plain boiled noodles.
Serves 6

Sauté de Veau aux Champignons
Veal in Cream and Mushroom Sauce

4 × 125 g (4 oz)
  veal escalopes,
  beaten
salt and pepper
25 g (1 oz) butter
1 clove garlic, crushed
250 g (8 oz)
  mushrooms, sliced
150 ml (¼ pint)
  Madeira or
  Marsala
150 ml (¼ pint)
  double cream
croûtes (heart-
  shaped) to garnish*

Season the veal with salt and pepper to taste. Melt the butter in a large frying pan, add the garlic and mushrooms and fry until soft. Remove and set aside. Add the veal and cook for 3 minutes on each side, until just tender. Pour in the Madeira or Marsala and cook for 3 minutes. Add the cream and mushrooms; simmer until thickened.

Arrange the veal on a warmed serving dish, spoon over the sauce and arrange the croûtes around the edge. Serve hot.
Serves 4

POULTRY & GAME

Poulet à l'Estragon
Chicken with Tarragon

25 g (1 oz) butter,
   softened
1 tablespoon chopped
   tarragon
1 clove garlic, crushed
salt and pepper
1 × 1.5 kg (3 lb)
   oven-ready chicken
1 tablespoon olive oil
2 tablespoons brandy
150 ml (¼ pint)
   double cream

TO GARNISH:
tarragon sprigs
heart-shaped croûtes*

Mix together the butter, tarragon, garlic, with salt and pepper to taste, and place inside the chicken. Place, breast down, in a roasting pan and cook in a preheated moderate oven, 180°C (350°F), Gas Mark 4, for 45 minutes.

Turn the chicken onto its back, baste with the cooking juices, and spoon over the olive oil. Return to the oven for 45 minutes, until tender.

Pour over the brandy and ignite. When the flames have died down, pour over the cream and mix with the juices. Return to the oven for 15 minutes.

Transfer to a warmed serving dish, garnish with tarragon and croûtes and serve immediately.
Serves 4

Coq au Vin de Bourgogne
Chicken in Red Wine

125 g (4 oz) streaky
  bacon, derinded
  and chopped
50 g (2 oz) butter
1 × 1.75 kg (4 lb)
  chicken, skinned
  and cut into
  serving pieces
12 shallots
6-8 tablespoons
  brandy (optional)
1 bottle red
  Burgundy wine
3 cloves garlic,
  crushed
1 bouquet garni*
1 bay leaf
salt and pepper
125 g (4 oz) button
  mushrooms
2 tablespoons plain
  flour

Lightly fry the bacon in its own fat
in a flameproof casserole, until
golden brown; remove from the pan.

Melt half the butter in the pan, add
the chicken and fry until browned all
over. Drain off excess fat. Add the
shallots and sauté for 2 to 3 minutes.

Remove from the heat. Pour in the
brandy, if using, ignite and leave
until the flames have died down.
Add the wine, garlic, bouquet garni,
bay leaf, and salt and pepper to taste.
Bring to the boil, cover and simmer
for 1 hour. Add the mushrooms and
cook for a further 15 minutes.

Blend the remaining butter with
the flour to make a *beurre manié**.
Remove the bouquet garni and bay
leaf from the casserole. Stir in
sufficient *beurre manié* to thicken the
sauce. Serve immediately.
Serves 6

Poulet aux Gousses D'Ail

Chicken with 30 Garlic Cloves

Don't be alarmed by the amount of garlic used – it imparts a delicate, rather than strong, flavour to the chicken.

30 cloves garlic
4 tablespoons olive oil
1 × 1.75 kg (4 lb) chicken, cut into serving pieces
1 bouquet garni* (parsley, thyme, sage, rosemary)
1 bay leaf
salt and pepper
grated nutmeg
2 tablespoons brandy
TO SERVE:
Pommes de Terre à la Provençale (see page 74)

Put the garlic in a casserole and spoon over half the oil. Put the chicken and herbs on top. Season liberally with salt, pepper and nutmeg. Cover and cook in a preheated moderate oven, 160°C (325°F), Gas Mark 3, for 45 minutes.

Turn the chicken pieces and add the remaining oil. Cover and return to the oven for 45 minutes.

Pour over the brandy, ignite and immediately cover; leave for 5 minutes.

Transfer the chicken to a warmed serving dish; keep hot. Strain the liquor into a small pan, discarding the garlic. Stir 1 tablespoon hot water into the residue in the casserole. Add to the liquor and bring to the boil. Pour a little over the chicken. Use the remainder to make the accompaniment. Serve hot.
Serves 6

Poulet Chasseur
Chicken with Vermouth and Tomatoes

50 g (2 oz) butter
1 × 1.75 kg (4 lb)
  chicken, cut into
  serving pieces
125 g (4 oz) baby
  onions
250 g (8 oz)
  shallots, chopped
150 ml (¼ pint) dry
  vermouth
1 bouquet garni*
1 bay leaf
salt and pepper
1 × 397 g (14 oz)
  can tomatoes
250 g (8 oz) button
  mushrooms
1 tablespoon tomato
  purée

Melt the butter in a pan, add the chicken pieces and fry until browned on all sides. Remove from the pan.

Add the onions and shallots to the pan and cook for 5 minutes.

Remove the pan from the heat, add the vermouth and ignite. When the flames have died down, return the chicken to the pan and add the bouquet garni, bay leaf, and salt and pepper to taste. Add the tomatoes with their juice, bring to the boil, cover and simmer for 1 hour.

Add the mushrooms and tomato purée and cook, uncovered, for 20 to 30 minutes, until the sauce is reduced and thickened. Serve immediately.

Serves 6

Canard au Poivre
Duck with Peppercorns

2 × 1 kg (2 lb)
  oven-ready
  ducklings
salt and pepper
25 g (1 oz) butter
4 shallots, finely
  chopped
150 ml (¼ pint) dry
  white wine
4 tablespoons brandy
4 tablespoons whole
  green peppercorns
  or 1 tablespoon
  black peppercorns,
  coarsely crushed
400 ml (14 fl oz)
  double cream

Prick the skin of the ducklings with a
fork and season liberally with salt
and pepper. Place in a roasting pan
and cook in a preheated moderately
hot oven, 200°C (400°F), Gas Mark
6, for about 1¼ hours until tender.

Meanwhile, melt the butter in a
pan, add the shallots and cook until
transparent. Stir in the wine and
brandy, bring to the boil and boil for
5 minutes.

Cut the ducklings into pieces,
arrange on a warmed serving dish
and keep hot. Add the peppercorns
and cream to the sauce and season
with salt to taste. Cook for 3 to 5
minutes until thickened.

Spoon the sauce over the
ducklings and serve immediately.
Serves 6

Pigeons en Estouffade
Stewed Pigeons

6 rashers streaky
  bacon, derinded
3 young pigeons,
  cleaned
50 g (2 oz) butter
2 tablespoons brandy
150 ml (¼ pint) dry
  white wine
10 pickling onions
6 tablespoons Fonds
  Brun (see page
  13) or beef stock
salt and pepper
125 g (4 oz) button
  mushrooms
1 tablespoon chopped
  parsley
TO GARNISH:
12-16 green olives
thyme sprigs

Wrap 2 rashers bacon around each
pigeon and secure with string. Melt
the butter in a pan, add the pigeons
and cook for 10 minutes until
browned all over. Pour over the
brandy and wine, bring to the boil
and cook for 2 minutes. Add the
onions, *fonds brun* or stock, and salt
and pepper to taste. Cover and
simmer for 1 hour. Add the
mushrooms and parsley and cook for
5 minutes.

Transfer to a warmed serving dish,
garnish with olives and thyme; serve
immediately.
Serves 6

Dindonneau Farci aux Marrons

Turkey with Chestnut and Apple Stuffing

500 g (1 lb)
    chestnuts
4 shallots, finely
    chopped
1 tablespoon chopped
    parsley
1 small egg, beaten
salt and pepper
500 g (1 lb) dessert
    apples, peeled,
    cored and chopped
250 g (8 oz) belly
    pork, finely
    chopped
1 × 5.5 kg (12 lb)
    oven-ready turkey
50 g (2 oz) butter
150 ml (¼ pint)
    Madeira
TO GARNISH:
apple rings
watercress sprigs

Cook the chestnuts in boiling water for 15 minutes. Drain, cool, skin and chop. Mix with the shallots, parsley, egg, and salt and pepper to taste.

Place the apples in a pan and cook, stirring, for 5 minutes. Mix into the stuffing, with the pork. Put the stuffing into the neck cavity of the turkey, then sew up the opening.

Place the turkey in a roasting pan, rub the skin with the butter, and season liberally with salt and pepper. Roast in a preheated moderate oven, 180°C (350°F), Gas Mark 4, basting occasionally, for 3½ to 4 hours.

Transfer the turkey to a warmed serving dish. Add the Madeira to the roasting pan, place over high heat and boil for 3 minutes. Spoon over the turkey and serve, garnished with apple rings and watercress.

Serves 10

Faisan en Casserole
Casseroled Pheasant with Port

125 g (4 oz) butter
1 large pheasant,
 quartered
2 large onions,
 chopped
1 clove garlic,
 crushed
450 ml (¾ pint)
 Fonds Brun (see
 page 13) or beef
 stock
grated rind and juice
 of 1 orange
150 ml (¼ pint)
 port
1 bay leaf
1 bouquet garni*
salt and pepper
2 tablespoons plain
 flour

Melt half the butter in a flameproof casserole, add the pheasant and fry until browned on all sides; remove from the pan.

Add the onions and garlic to the pan and cook gently for 10 minutes. Return the pheasant to the pan, add the *fonds brun* or beef stock, orange rind and juice, port, herbs, and salt and pepper to taste. Bring to the boil, then cook in a preheated moderate oven, 160°C (325°F), Gas Mark 3, for 2½ hours, until tender.

Transfer the pheasant to a warmed serving dish; keep hot. Blend the remaining butter with the flour to make a *beurre manié**. Place the roasting pan over high heat and add sufficient *beurre manié* to thicken the sauce. Spoon over the pheasant to serve.
Serves 4

Lapin à la Moutarde
Rabbit with Mustard

*1 × 1.5 kg (3 lb)
  rabbit*
*300 ml (½ pint) dry
  white wine*
2 onions, chopped
3 carrots, chopped
few parsley sprigs
1 bouquet garni*
1 clove garlic, crushed
2 cloves
salt and pepper
*6 rashers streaky
  bacon*
*2 tablespoons French
  mustard*
*thyme sprigs to
  garnish*

Put the rabbit in a large dish, add the wine, onions, carrots, herbs, garlic, cloves, and salt and pepper to taste. Leave to marinate for 12 hours, stirring occasionally. Drain well, reserving the liquid.

Wrap the bacon around the rabbit and secure with string. Spread with the mustard and place in a roasting pan. Cook in a preheated moderate oven, 180°C (350°F), Gas Mark 4, for about 1½ hours until tender, basting occasionally.

Place the rabbit on a warmed serving dish, remove the string, and keep warm. Add the reserved marinade to the roasting pan. Place over a high heat and boil for 5 minutes. Spoon over the rabbit and garnish with thyme to serve.
Serves 4 to 6

Haricots Verts à la Française
French-Style Green Beans

100 g (3½ oz)
   butter
2 bunches spring
   onions, cut into
   5 cm (2 inch)
   lengths
1 kg (2 lb) small
   French beans,
   topped and tailed
salt and pepper
1 crisp lettuce,
   quartered
1 bunch of mixed
   herbs (including
   parsley and
   chervil), tied
   together

Melt the butter in a pan, add the spring onions and cook for 2 minutes. Add the beans and cook for 20 minutes. Season with salt and pepper to taste. Add the lettuce and herbs and cook for 5 minutes.

Remove the herbs and transfer to a warmed serving dish. Serve immediately.

Serves 4

Oignons Glacés
Glazed Onions

8 cloves
8 medium onions,
   peeled
300 ml (½ pint)
   Fonds Brun, (see
   page 13) or beef
   stock
salt and pepper
25 g (1 oz) butter,
   melted
8 sugar lumps
1 tablespoon caster
   sugar

Push a clove into the base of each onion. Place in a greased ovenproof dish and spoon over the *fonds brun* or stock. Season with salt and pepper to taste and spoon over the butter. Bake in a preheated moderate oven, 160°C (325°F), Gas Mark 3, for 1¼ to 1½ hours until tender.

Place a sugar lump on each onion and sprinkle with caster sugar. Cook under a preheated hot grill until the sugar is caramelized. Serve hot, with roast or grilled meat.

Serves 4

Cèpes Farcis
Stuffed Mushrooms

8 large flat
   mushrooms
50 g (2 oz) butter
1 slice white bread,
   crusts removed
1 tablespoon chopped
   parsley
1 clove garlic,
   crushed
4 shallots, chopped
salt and pepper
4 tablespoons dry
   white wine
parsley sprigs to
   garnish

Remove the mushroom stalks and chop them finely. Melt half the butter in a pan, add the mushroom caps and cook for 5 minutes. Remove from the pan and set aside.

Soak the bread in water for a few minutes, then squeeze almost dry and place in a basin.

Melt the remaining butter in the pan, add the chopped mushroom stalks, parsley, garlic and shallots and cook for 5 minutes. Season with salt and pepper to taste and pour in the wine. Increase the heat and cook for 2 minutes. Stir into the bread.

Arrange the mushroom caps in an ovenproof dish and fill with the mixture. Cover and cook in a preheated moderate oven, 180°C (350°F), Gas Mark 4, for 20 minutes. Serve hot, garnished with parsley.
Serves 4

Artichauts Cailloux
Stuffed Artichoke Hearts

6 large young
   artichokes, stalks
   removed
salt and pepper
50 g (2 oz) butter
175 g (6 oz) button
   mushrooms,
   chopped
250 g (8 oz) lean
   ham, chopped
1 tablespoon chopped
   parsley
1 teaspoon curry
   powder
150 ml (¼ pint) hot
   Sauce Mornay
   (see page 17)
125 g (4 oz) Gruyère
   cheese, grated

Cook the artichokes in boiling salted water for 30 to 35 minutes or until tender. Drain and allow to cool. Remove the outside leaves and choke.

Place the artichoke hearts in a greased ovenproof dish. Season with salt and pepper to taste.

Melt the butter in a pan, add the mushrooms and cook for 7 minutes. Add the ham and parsley and heat gently. Stir the curry powder into the *sauce mornay*. Add the mushroom mixture and mix well. Pile on top of the artichokes.

Sprinkle with cheese and bake in a preheated moderately hot oven, 190°C (375°F), Gas Mark 5, for 15 to 20 minutes, until golden.
Serves 4 to 6

Charlotte d'Aubergines

1 kg (2 lb)
  aubergines, sliced
salt
50 g (2 oz) butter
1 large onion, sliced
2 cloves garlic,
  crushed
500 g (1 lb)
  tomatoes, skinned
  and chopped
4 tablespoons oil
300 g (10 oz)
  natural low-fat
  yogurt
150 ml (¼ pint)
  chicken stock

Sprinkle the aubergine slices with salt and leave to stand for 30 minutes. Rinse under cold water and dry well.

Melt the butter in a pan, add the onion and garlic and fry until lightly browned. Stir in the tomatoes and cook for 20 to 25 minutes, until thickened.

Heat the oil in another pan and fry the aubergine slices until browned on both sides. Drain on kitchen paper.

Line the base and sides of a 1.5 litre (2½ pint) Charlotte mould with aubergine slices. Fill with layers of tomato mixture, yogurt and aubergines, finishing with aubergines.

Cover with foil and cook in a preheated moderate oven, 180°C (350°F), Gas Mark 4, for 40 to 45 minutes, until tender. Leave for 10 minutes, then turn out onto a warmed serving dish.

Heat any remaining tomato sauce with the stock and spoon around the Charlotte. Serve immediately.
Serves 4 to 6

Pommes Lyonnaise

Potatoes Lyonnaise

40 g (1½ oz) butter
500 g (1 lb) onions,
  finely sliced
1 kg (2 lb) potatoes,
  finely sliced
salt and pepper
2 tablespoons
  chopped parsley

Melt the butter in a pan, add the onions and fry until golden.

Arrange the potatoes and onions in layers in an ovenproof dish, sprinkling each layer liberally with salt and pepper and the parsley. Cover and cook in a preheated moderate oven, 180°C (350°F), Gas Mark 4, for 1 to 1¼ hours until the potatoes are tender. Serve hot.
Serves 4 to 6

Pommes de Terre à l'Ail

Potatoes with Cheese and Bacon

2 tablespoons olive
   oil
175 g (6 oz) streaky
   bacon, derinded
   and chopped
1 kg (2 lb) potatoes,
   thinly sliced
150 g (5 oz) Gruyère
   cheese, grated
salt and pepper
3 cloves garlic,
   crushed
2 tablespoons
   chopped parsley
4 tablespoons double
   cream

Heat the oil in a heavy-based pan, add the bacon and fry until golden and crisp.

Arrange the potatoes, cheese and bacon in layers in a greased ovenproof dish, seasoning each layer with salt and pepper to taste. Sprinkle the top with garlic and parsley.

Cover and cook in a preheated moderately hot oven, 190°C (375°F), Gas Mark 5, for 45 to 50 minutes. Pour over the cream, cover and return to the oven for 5 minutes. Serve immediately.

Serves 4 to 6

Pommes de Terre à la Provençale

Mediterranean Potato Dish

This dish is delicious with roast or cold meats. If you are making *Poulet aux gousses d'ail* (see page 64) use the garlic residue in place of the garlic stock prepared here.

½ head garlic cloves,
   unpeeled
1 bouquet garni*
300 ml (½ pint)
   water
8 potatoes, thickly
   sliced
4 large tomatoes,
   skinned, seeded
   and sliced
salt and pepper
chopped parsley to
   garnish

Place the garlic, bouquet garni and water in a pan and simmer for 20 to 30 minutes. Cool, remove both from the pan, discard the bouquet garni and peel the garlic. Pound the garlic in a mortar with the water from the pan until smooth.

Spoon half the garlic residue into a small ovenproof dish. Arrange the potatoes and tomatoes in layers on top and season well with salt and pepper. Spoon over the remaining garlic residue.

Cover and cook in a preheated moderate oven, 180°C (350°F), Gas Mark 4, for 1 to 1¼ hours, until the potatoes are tender. Serve garnished with parsley.

Serves 4 to 6

Chou Rouge aux Saucisses Landais

Red Cabbage with Sausages

1 medium red
   cabbage, finely
   sliced
500 g (1 lb) cooking
   apples, cored and
   diced
500 g (1 lb) onions,
   sliced
2 green peppers,
   cored, seeded and
   sliced
grated rind of
   ½ small orange
2 cloves garlic,
   crushed
salt and pepper
grated nutmeg
175 ml (6 fl oz) dry
   red wine
150 ml (¼ pint)
   wine vinegar
500 g (1 lb) cooked
   smoked sausage

Layer the cabbage, apples, onions and peppers in a casserole. Sprinkle with the orange rind, garlic, and salt, pepper and nutmeg to taste. Repeat until all the ingredients are used. Pour over the wine and vinegar.

Cover and cook in a preheated moderate oven, 160°C (325°F), Gas Mark 3, for 2 hours.

Cut the sausage into 2.5 cm (1 inch) slices. Add to the casserole and spoon the cabbage over them. Cook for 1½ hours. Serve hot, with boiled potatoes or pasta.

Serves 4 to 6

Ratatouille

2 tablespoons olive
   oil
2 cloves garlic,
   crushed
2 large onions, sliced
2 aubergines, sliced
6 courgettes, sliced
   diagonally
1 green pepper,
   cored, seeded and
   sliced
750 g (1½ lb)
   tomatoes, skinned
   and sliced
salt and pepper
2 tablespoons tomato
   purée

Heat the oil in a pan, add the garlic and onions and cook for 5 minutes, stirring occasionally. Add the aubergines, courgettes and pepper and stir in the tomatoes. Season with salt and pepper to taste, bring to the boil and simmer for 20 minutes. Add the tomato purée and cook for 10 minutes. Serve hot or cold.

Serves 4 to 6

Poireaux Vinaigrette

Leeks Vinaigrette

6 leeks
1 tablespoon chopped
   capers
DRESSING:
2 tablespoons lemon
   juice
4 tablespoons olive
   oil
1 teaspoon caster
   sugar
1 teaspoon Meaux
   mustard
1 clove garlic, crushed
salt and pepper
1 tablespoon each
   chopped parsley
   and chives

Slice the leeks very finely and arrange in a salad bowl.

Put the dressing ingredients in a screw-topped jar and shake well. Pour over the leeks, add the capers and toss well. Chill for 1 hour before serving.

Serves 4

Salade aux Artichauts

Rice and Artichoke Salad

175 g (6 oz)
    long-grain rice
salt
25 g (1 oz) butter
1 clove garlic,
    crushed
1 onion, finely
    chopped
50 g (2 oz) button
    mushrooms, sliced
1 × 397 g (14 oz)
    can artichoke
    hearts, drained
2 tablespoons
    chopped parsley
DRESSING:
2 tablespoons lemon
    juice
4 tablespoons olive
    oil
1 clove garlic, crushed
1/2 teaspoon sugar
1/2 teaspoon French
    mustard

Cook the rice in boiling salted water for 12 to 14 minutes until just tender. Drain well and allow to cool.

Melt the butter in a pan, add the garlic and onion and fry until golden. Add the mushrooms and cook for 2 minutes. Stir into the rice.

Cut the artichoke hearts in half and add to the rice mixture with the parsley.

Put the dressing ingredients in a screw-topped jar and shake well. Pour over the salad and mix well. Turn into a salad bowl and serve immediately.
Serves 4 to 6

Salade de Haricots Blanc
Haricot Bean and Tuna Salad

½ lettuce
4 large tomatoes,
    chopped
50 g (2 oz) black
    olives, stoned and
    halved
1 clove garlic, crushed
8 tablespoons haricot
    beans, cooked
3 hard-boiled eggs,
    quartered
1 × 198 g (7 oz)
    can tuna fish,
    drained
DRESSING:
3 tablespoons olive
    oil
1 ½ tablespoons white
    wine vinegar
salt and pepper
½ teaspoon French
    mustard
TO GARNISH:
chopped chives

Arrange the lettuce in a large salad
bowl and pile the remaining salad
ingredients on top.

Put the dressing ingredients in a
screw-topped jar and shake well.
Pour over the salad and toss well.

Sprinkle with chives and serve
immediately.

Serves 4

DESSERTS

Mousse à l'Orange

6 eggs, separated
175 g (6 oz) caster
   sugar
3 tablespoons
   Cointreau
grated rind and juice
   of 4 oranges
15 g (½ oz) gelatine
2 tablespoons water
150 ml (¼ pint)
   double cream,
   lightly whipped
mint leaves to
   decorate

Put the egg yolks and sugar in a bowl over a pan of hot water and whisk until thick and creamy. Gradually whisk in the Cointreau, orange rind and juice. Continue whisking until the mixture is thick. Remove from the heat and allow to cool slightly.

Put the gelatine and water in a bowl over a pan of hot water and stir until dissolved. Add to the orange mixture. Fold in the cream. Whisk the egg whites until stiff and fold into the orange mixture.

Spoon into individual dishes and chill until set.

Decorate with mint to serve.

Serves 6

NOTE: For a professional finish, serve the mousse in scooped out orange shells, as shown.

Petits Pots de Café

25 g (1 oz) butter
2 tablespoons caster
    sugar
1 tablespoon rum
2 teaspoons powdered
    instant coffee
3 eggs, separated
TO DECORATE:
120 ml (4 fl oz)
    double cream,
    whipped
few walnut halves

Put the butter, sugar, rum and coffee in a bowl over a pan of hot water and stir until melted. Add the egg yolks and mix well. Leave to cook over the hot water for 5 minutes, stirring occasionally. Remove from the heat and cool.

Whisk the egg whites until stiff, then fold into the coffee mixture. Spoon into individual ramekins and decorate each with piped cream and walnuts.
Serves 4

Vacherin

SWISS MERINGUE:
4 egg whites
250 g (8 oz) caster
sugar
½ teaspoon vanilla
essence

ITALIAN MERINGUE:
250 g (8 oz) caster
sugar
150 ml (¼ pint)
water
4 egg whites

FILLING:
284 ml (10 fl oz)
double cream
1 tablespoon caster
sugar
1 teaspoon vanilla
essence
250-350 g (8-12 oz)
fresh strawberries
or raspberries

To make the Swiss meringue: Whisk the egg whites until stiff.. Gradually whisk in the sugar and add the vanilla essence. Spoon into a piping bag fitted with a 2.5 cm (1 inch) plain nozzle. Pipe 20 fingers 10 cm (4 inches) long onto a baking sheet.

Draw an 18 to 20 cm (7 to 8 inch) circle on non-stick paper and spread with the remaining meringue. Bake the meringue fingers and circle in a preheated very cool oven, 120°C (250°F), Gas Mark ½, for 1 to 1½ hours, until crisp and pale golden. To make the Italian meringue: Heat the sugar and water gently until dissolved. Bring to the boil, and continue boiling until 120°C (250°F) is registered on a sugar thermometer.

Whisk the egg whites until stiff. Gradually pour in the hot syrup, whisking all the time; continue whisking until the meringue is cold.

Spoon into a piping bag fitted with a 2.5 cm (1 inch) star nozzle, and pipe a row of stars just inside the edge of the meringue circle. Stand the meringue fingers upright on the stars, rounded side outwards. Pipe Italian meringue between the fingers inside and outside to hold them in place. Decorate with the remaining meringue. Return to the oven for 1 hour, until the meringue base and fingers are crisp. The Italian meringue remains slightly soft and sticky. Allow to cool.

Whip the cream and sugar together until stiff and add the vanilla essence. Pile into the meringue case and top with fruit. Serve chilled.

Serves 6 to 8
NOTE: Do not fill this dessert more than 2 hours before required.

Mont Blanc

2 egg whites
125 g (4 oz) caster
  sugar
½ teaspoon vanilla
  eseence
FILLING:
150 ml (¼ pint)
  double cream
1 tablespoon icing
  sugar
1 × 227 g (8 oz)
  can sweetened
  chestnut purée
1 tablespoon brandy
25 g (1 oz) plain
  chocolate, grated

Whisk the egg whites until stiff.
Gradually whisk in the caster sugar
and ¼ teaspoon vanilla essence.
Spoon the meringue into a piping
bag fitted with a 1 cm (½ inch) plain
nozzle. Draw 4 circles 7.5 cm
(3 inches) in diameter onto baking
sheets lined with non-stick paper and
cover with the meringue.

Bake in a preheated very cool
oven, 120°C (250°F), Gas Mark ½,
for about 1¼ hours, until firm but
not browned. Cool. Arrange on
serving plates.

Whip the cream until it forms soft
peaks, then fold in the icing sugar
and remaining vanilla essence.

Mix the chestnut purée with the
brandy. Spoon into a piping bag
fitted with a 3 mm (⅛ inch) plain
nozzle and pipe around the edge of
the meringue bases. Top with the
cream and chocolate. Serve chilled.
Serves 4

Gâteau de Noisettes aux Fruits

Hazelnut and Fruit Torte

PASTRY:
150 g (5 oz) plain
   flour
pinch of salt
250 g (8 oz)
   hazelnuts, ground
125 g (4 oz) caster
   sugar
125 g (4 oz) butter,
   softened
1 egg yolk

FILLING:
284 ml (10 fl oz)
   double cream,
   whipped
1 fresh pineapple,
   peeled, cored and
   sliced

Sift the flour and salt onto a board, make a well in the centre and put in the hazelnuts, sugar, butter and egg yolk. Work the flour into the centre, using the fingers; mix to a smooth paste. Cover and chill for 1 hour.

Divide the dough into 3 pieces. Roll out each piece and use to line the bases of three 20 cm (8 inch) flan rings, placed on baking sheets. Prick with a fork. Mark one round into 8 triangles. Bake in a preheated moderately hot oven, 190°C (375°F), Gas Mark 5, for 10 minutes or until golden brown. Break the marked round into triangles. Cool.

Put one circle on a serving dish and spread with a layer of cream. Top with half the pineapple, cover with the other round and spread with cream.

Decorate with the remaining cream: pipe 8 lines radiating from the centre, place the pastry triangles on these and top with the remaining pineapple. Finish with cream rosettes.

Serves 8

Les Bourdaines
Apples Baked in Pastry

PÂTE SABLÉE:
250 g (8 oz) plain
    flour
pinch of salt
125 g (4 oz) butter
1 tablespoon caster
    sugar
3-5 tablespoons iced
    water
4 large dessert
    apples, peeled and
    cored
4 tablespoons quince
    or plum jam
beaten egg to glaze

Sift the flour and salt into a bowl. Rub in the butter until the mixture resembles fine breadcrumbs, then stir in the sugar. Mix in enough water to give a smooth, pliable dough.

Divide the dough into 4 pieces and roll each into a square. Fill the centres of the apples with the jam and place on the squares.

Brush the edges of the squares with water and wrap the pastry around the apples. Trim any excess pastry and press the edges firmly to seal. Decorate with pastry leaves cut from the trimmings.

Place on a baking sheet and brush with beaten egg. Bake in a preheated moderate oven, 160°C (325°F), Gas Mark 3, for 20 to 25 minutes until golden brown. Serve hot, with cream.
Serves 4

Babas au Rhum
Rum Babas

15 g (½ oz) dried
   yeast
2 tablespoons
   lukewarm water
pinch of caster sugar
250 g (8 oz) strong
   plain flour
1 tablespoon sugar
3 eggs
½ teaspoon salt
75 g (3 oz) currants
6 tablespoons rum
100 g (3½ oz)
   butter, softened
250 g (8 oz)
   granulated sugar
scant 900 ml
   (1½ pints) water
250 g (8 oz) fresh
   strawberries,
   raspberries or
   cherries to serve

Mix the yeast with the water and caster sugar and leave for about 10 minutes until frothy.

Put the flour and sugar in a bowl and make a well in the centre. Add the yeast mixture. Break in the eggs and add the salt. Work to a smooth, elastic dough. Cover and leave in a warm place until doubled in bulk. Meanwhile, soak the currants in 2 tablespoons of the rum.

Knead the butter and currants into the dough. Spoon into 8 small greased baba tins, cover and leave in a warm place for 45 to 50 minutes, until the dough has risen to 5 mm (¼ inch) below the top of the tins. Bake in a preheated moderately hot oven, 200°C (400°F), Gas Mark 6, for 15 to 20 minutes, until golden; cool.

Heat the granulated sugar and water in a pan until dissolved, then boil for 3 to 4 minutes until slightly thickened and clear. Stir in the remaining rum and spoon over the babas. Fill with fruit to serve.
Makes 8

Crêpes aux Fraises
Strawberry Crêpes

125 g (4 oz) plain
flour, sifted
pinch of salt
1 teaspoon caster
sugar
1 egg
1 egg yolk
4 tablespoons milk
2 tablespoons water
2 tablespoons melted
butter
250 g (8 oz) fresh
strawberries, sliced
50 g (2 oz) icing
sugar, sifted
4 tablespoons brandy
25 g (1 oz) butter

Put the flour, salt and sugar in a
bowl. Make a well in the centre and
add the egg and yolk. Mix well.

Gradually beat in the milk and
water, stir in the melted butter and
mix well. Leave for at least 2 hours.

Meanwhile mix the strawberries,
icing sugar and 1 tablespoon of the
brandy together. Chill for 1 hour.

Stir the batter well; if necessary
add more water to give a thin batter.
Lightly grease a 13–18 cm (6–7 inch)
frying pan with butter and place over
a moderate heat. Cook 12 crêpes in
the usual way (see *Gateau de crêpes à
la florentine*, page 34); keep hot.

Divide the strawberry mixture
between the crêpes. Fold into
quarters and arrange in a buttered
flambé or shallow ovenproof dish.
Dot with butter and bake in a preheated moderately hot oven, 200°C
(400°F), Gas Mark 6, for 10 minutes.

Warm the remaining brandy, pour
over the crêpes, ignite and serve.
Serves 6

Soufflé Praline

1 tablespoon plain
  flour
150 ml (¼ pint)
  milk
50 g (2 oz) vanilla
  sugar*
4 eggs, separated
25 g (1 oz) butter,
  softened
PRALINE:
40 g (1½ oz)
  almonds, chopped
40 g (1½ oz)
  hazelnuts,
  chopped
75 g (3 oz)
  granulated sugar
2 tablespoons water

To make the praline: Put the nuts on a baking sheet and place under a preheated moderate grill until lightly browned; cool. Put the sugar and water in a small pan and boil until the sugar caramelizes. Stir in the nuts and pour immediately onto an oiled baking sheet. Leave until cold, then pound to a coarse powder in a mortar.

Beat the flour with 2 tablespoons of the milk in a pan until smooth. Add the remaining milk and sugar. Slowly bring to the boil, stirring. Cook for 1 minute.

Beat in the egg yolks, one at a time. Stir in the butter. Cool, then stir in the praline. Whisk the egg whites until stiff and fold into the mixture.

Turn into a 1.2-1.5 litre (2-2½ pint) buttered soufflé dish. Cook in a preheated moderately hot oven, 190°C (375°F), Gas Mark 5, for 35 to 40 minutes, until risen and golden. Serve immediately.
Serves 4 to 6

Profiteroles au Caramel

CHOUX PASTRY:
*150 ml (¼ pint)
    water*
50 g (2 oz) butter
*65 g (2½ oz) plain
    flour*
pinch of salt
2 eggs, lightly beaten
FILLING:
*250 ml (8 fl oz)
    double cream,
    lightly whipped*
CARAMEL SAUCE:
*75 g (3 oz)
    granulated sugar*
*4 tablespoons cold
    water*
*150 ml (¼ pint)
    double cream*

Put the water and butter in a pan and bring to the boil. Take off the heat, add the flour and salt and beat until the paste is smooth and forms a ball. Cool slightly, then gradually beat in the eggs, to form a smooth shiny paste.

Spoon into a piping bag fitted with a 2.5 cm (1 inch) plain nozzle and pipe small mounds on greased baking sheets. Bake in a preheated moderately hot oven, 200°C (400°F), Gas Mark 6, for 15 to 20 minutes, until risen and golden.

Transfer to a wire rack and split each one. Cool, then fill with cream.

Heat the sugar in a pan over low heat until dissolved. Increase the heat and cook to a golden brown caramel. Remove from the heat and carefully add the water. Return to the heat and stir until the caramel dissolves. Cool, then whip into the cream.

Arrange the profiteroles on a dish and spoon over the sauce. Serve chilled.

Serves 6

Tartelettes aux Fruits

PASTRY:
175 g (6 oz) plain
flour
pinch of salt
65 g (2½ oz) caster
sugar
3 egg yolks
100 g (3½ oz)
butter, softened
FILLING:
4 tablespoons
redcurrant jelly
1 tablespoon water
350-500 g (12 oz-
1 lb) prepared
fresh fruit, (e.g.
strawberries,
raspberries,
grapes, cherries,
apricots,
tangerines)

Sift the flour onto a pastry board and make a well in the centre. Put the salt, sugar and egg yolks into the well and gradually work into the flour until smooth. Quickly knead in the butter. Form into a ball, cover and chill for 1 hour.

Roll out the pastry and use to line eight 7.5 cm (3 inch) tartlet tins; chill for 20 minutes. Bake blind* in a preheated moderately hot oven, 200°C (400°F), Gas Mark 6, for 10 to 12 minutes, until the pastry is golden brown; cool.

Stir the redcurrant jelly with the water in a pan over low heat until blended. Brush the bases of the pastry cases with this glaze. Arrange the fruit on top as desired and brush with glaze. Serve with cream.
Makes 8

Omelette Soufflé au Grand Marnier

6 macaroons
4 tablespoons Grand
Marnier
100 g (3½ oz)
*vanilla sugar**
5 eggs, separated

Carefully dip the macaroons into the liqueur. Arrange in the base of a gratin dish. Sprinkle over any remaining Grand Marnier and 1 tablespoon sugar.

Beat the egg yolks and remaining sugar until thick and creamy. Whisk the egg whites until stiff and fold into the yolk mixture. Spoon over the macaroons, and shape into a dome.

Make shallow slits over the surface to enable the heat to penetrate. Bake in a preheated moderately hot oven, 190°C (375°F), Gas Mark 5, for 20 minutes, until well risen and golden brown. Serve immediately.
Serves 6

Sorbet aux Pêches

500 g (1 lb) ripe
    peaches, skinned
    and stoned
2 ripe apricots,
    skinned and stoned
175 g (6 oz) caster
    sugar
juice of ½ lemon
6 tablespoons cold
    water
fresh peach slices to
    decorate

Work the fruit in an electric blender
or rub through a sieve until smooth.

Put the sugar, lemon juice and
water in a pan and heat, stirring,
until dissolved. Bring to the boil and
simmer for 2 minutes. Cool, then stir
into the purée.

Turn into a freezerproof container
and freeze for about 1 hour, until
small ice crystals have formed
around the edge. Whisk thoroughly,
then return to the container and
freeze for at least 6 to 8 hours.

Transfer to the refrigerator about 1
hour before serving, to soften
slightly. Spoon into serving dishes
and top with peach slices. Serve with
boudoir biscuits.
Serves 4

Glace au café
Coffee ice cream

150 ml (¼ pint)
  single cream
150 ml (¼ pint)
  strong coffee made
  from freshly
  ground coffee
  beans
4 egg yolks
100 g (4 oz) caster
  sugar
300 ml (½ pint)
  double cream
2 tablespoons iced
  water
langue de chat
  biscuits to serve
  (optional)

Place the single cream and coffee in a pan and warm gently until lukewarm. Remove from the heat and set aside.

Whisk the egg yolks and sugar together until the mixture is pale and thick. Whisk in the coffee cream and return the mixture to the pan. Heat gently, stirring constantly, until the custard thickens. Set aside to cool.

Whip the double cream with the water until it forms soft peaks. Add the coffee custard and beat lightly. Turn into a freezerproof container. Cover, seal and freeze until firm.

Transfer to the refrigerator 30 minutes before serving to soften. Scoop into chilled glasses and serve with langue de chat biscuits if liked.
Serves 4

Coupe Glacée aux Framboises
Raspberry ice cream sundae

350 g (12 oz)
  raspberries, fresh
  or frozen
juice of 1 orange
juice of 1 lemon
175 g (6 oz)
  granulated sugar
450 ml (¾ pint)
  double cream
3 tablespoons iced
  water
TO SERVE:
175 g (6 oz)
  raspberries
3 tablespoons Kirsch
  or Brandy
2 tablespoons toasted
  almonds

Rub the raspberries through a sieve or purée in an electric blender, then sieve to remove pips.

Mix the purée with the orange and lemon juices and the sugar. Chill in the refrigerator for about 1 hour.

Whip the cream with the water until it forms soft peaks. Stir in the raspberry purée and beat lightly together. Turn into a rigid freezer proof container. Cover, seal and freeze for 1 hour. Meanwhile, soak the raspberries in the liqueur.

Remove the ice cream from the freezer; stir, then freeze until solid.

Transfer to the refrigerator 30 minutes before serving to soften. Spoon half the raspberries into 4 chilled glasses and scoop the ice cream on top. Top with the remaining raspberries and almonds.
Serves 4

INDEX

Acknowledgments

Photography by Paul Williams
Food prepared by Caroline Ellwood
Designed by Astrid Publishing Consultants Ltd.